THE CAUSES OF HUMAN MISERY

REFLECTIONS

on

THE CAUSES OF
HUMAN MISERY

and upon

Certain Proposals

to Eliminate Them

BARRINGTON MOORE, JR.

Beacon Press   Boston

To E.C.M.

Anyone who writes a book, however gloomy its message may be, is necessarily an optimist. If the pessimists really believed what they were saying there would be no point in saying it.

Joan Robinson, *Freedom and Necessity*

Contents

Preface

Two centuries ago the title of this little book might have struck the ordinary reader as neither over long nor over bold. Today it smacks of *hubris*. Though the contrast reveals something about changes in the intellectual climate since the eighteenth century, it does not necessarily demonstrate the superiority of twentieth-century ways of perceiving and posing issues. Now, as well as then, it remains impossible to assess the causes of human misery and efforts to remove or reduce them in a way that could command assent among informed and thoughtful people with sharply contrasting political persuasions. Nevertheless an impossible task may remain one worth attempting, because mistakes and errors—as long as it is possible to demonstrate that they are mistakes—have long played a very significant role in the discovery of truth. Furthermore, there are grounds for suspecting that the task is not really quite as impossible as we are inclined to believe. Belief in the impossibility of agreement about painful issues is one way to avoid discussing them. It serves to protect beliefs against disagreeable scrutiny.

The author began this set of essays as an act of combined relaxation and self-discipline, doubting whether the result would require or deserve publication. Amid the current flood of books it seemed that the time might have returned when the circulation of handwritten manuscripts could be the more appropriate method of communication for the purpose at hand. That purpose was to set down in as coherent and orderly a manner as possible the most important things one scholar had learned about the causes of human misery. After studying a variety of their forms in many times and places for the better part of four decades it seemed to me that it would be rather odd if I could not make some sort of a synthesis of the more important points and give an indication of the reasoning behind them that would be useful to a few friends, colleagues, and students.

The challenge of the task proved considerably more formidable than originally anticipated. The length of time and number of pages required to achieve some degree of clarity grew continually as the work proceeded. By itself this fact would scarcely justify presenting these pages to a larger audience. However, I gradually became aware that the perplexities facing me were very likely a somewhat concentrated version of those facing others. The accidents of my life and reading have at various points in time brought me into sustained and close contact with views of human nature and society that span the political spectrum all the way from thoroughly reactionary through liberal to extremist radical. I have studied Herbert Spencer as carefully as Herbert Marcuse. Though I do count it as one of the most fortunate accidents of my life that the latter rather than the former has long been a close friend, both have had a meaningful impact upon my way of asking questions and seeking relevant evidence for their answers. The obligation to make sense of this rather varied intellectual precipitate is a task that many people feel in some degree that they ought to execute. In an age of unavoidable specialization and scarcely less avoidable rancor such attempts at synthesis become all the more necessary. They are efforts to perceive the whole through critical interpretations of the evidence that partial perspectives provide. If this small book helps others with similar purposes, it will have achieved at least one of its author's objectives. In my own form of this attempt I have done my best to steer clear of mere advocacy of any particular political position, least of all any currently fashionable one. Instead, there is an effort to assess arguments impartially and let the political chips fall where they will.

Such an undertaking is like trying to live in an old house, continuously occupied over a long period of time and furnished by successive generations of occupants with widely differing tastes. Whether we know it or not, that is of course the actual situation every human being faces, because all of us live in a culture that is in a quite concrete sense the precipitate of past human experiences. In this situation there are three conceivable courses of action. One can continue to live amidst the accumulated jumble without more than dimly noticing that it *is* a jumble. Most people do this most of the time. Even professional thinkers probably live in this manner much more than they realize because their span of attention is necessarily limited and selective. At the opposite extreme one can throw out all of the old furniture and install a complete new set in the latest fashion . . . at least if one has the money, time, and taste. There is then of course the double risk that the latest fashion may soon seem rather absurd and that much will be discarded that has lasting value and can make the house both livable and beautiful. Furthermore, there are rather good reasons for holding that at the level of human culture and social organization this kind of total refurnishing is simply impossible. Finally, there is the third approach of rearranging this inherited furniture, deciding what to keep, what to discard, what items belong where, and why they belong there. For those who take intellectual life seriously and are not content to leave the inside of their heads in the state of a rummage sale or second-hand auction, this task is at the very least an intermittently recurring one. Whether there are any existing or even possible criteria that have always governed such rearrangements and always will, constitutes one of many questions I cannot answer, though my acquaintance with historical writings has given me the sense that, while the process remains the same, the criteria and plan of rearrangement undergo fundamental changes. In any event it is necessary at some point to be explicit about these criteria and the reasons for selection, rejection, and rearrangement. That is one of the tasks I have tried to perform, one which, even with its failures, may make the book helpful to a wider audience.

There is another and perhaps more important justification. The mere act of putting various theses into a coherent order, or even attempting to do so, has the consequence that one learns something about their validity. Logic, even in elementary forms, comes into play through the effort of setting down ideas and their justifications in their apparent relationship to each other. Doing so leads to the discovery of further questions that ought to be asked and answered. If this little book helps and stimulates others to supersede it by better questions with firmer answers, it will have really served its purpose. In this connection, however, a few words of pessimism may be in order. Every thinker and teacher from whom I have learned something has stressed the importance of facing up to unpleasant facts and disturbing theoretical conclusions. But it also appears to me that in their own work they faced up to conclusions that were unpleasant and disturbing to their intellectual opponents, seldom if ever to their own intellectual positions and views of the world.* This is true even in those instances of individuals who have courageously made the most severe personal sacrifices rather than abandon viewpoints and arguments they have struggled to reach by what I hold to be essentially valid intellectual processes.

The most creative minds, it appears, are one-track minds. Those who thrust human thought a few notches along paths that turn up new and important truths manage to exclude indications contrary to the general bent of their intellects or else absorb them in such a manner as to render these indications harmless. Those of us who

---

* Dredging my memory I can recall only one clearcut case of at least a moderately distinguished social scientist admitting that evidence showed his basic life's work to have been mistaken. That was Raymond Pearl, a demographer. (See Philip Hauser, ed., *The Study of Population: An Inventory and Appraisal* (Chicago and London, 1959), p. 160.) In some areas of inquiry it is possible and even likely that the investigator will at a fairly early stage come upon clues indicating that one is on the wrong track. Then it is possible to change over. That happens in varying degrees, depending upon both the subject matter and the temperament of the investigator. As such, however, the distinction is not one, as is popularly supposed, between "hard" areas such as physical science and "soft" ones such as social science. That much one can see very vividly in *Albert Einstein, Hedwig und Max Born: Briefwechsel 1916–1955* (Munich, 1969). There is also a brief but thought-provoking account of mathematicians' errors in assessing the work of another mathematician in C. P. Snow's introduction to G. H. Hardy, *A Mathematician's Apology* (Cambridge University Press, 1967), pp. 33–34. Aside from proving the banality that scientists are after all human, such instances merely show that the conception of science itself changes in response to scientific criticism. They do not provide a warrant for the rejection of scientific method in favor of some "higher" methods. To argue in that fashion would be to hold that errors in arithmetic and conceptual advances over simple arithmetic (as in algebra) would constitute grounds for rejecting the validity of arithmetic.

have much less creative talent can take comfort from the fact that these creative minds leave behind them a legacy that is scarcely an unmixed blessing. Just about as much human misery is traceable to the thoughts and behavior of geniuses as to that of the stupid and incompetent. Nor is it always a simple matter to draw a clear distinction between the two. In other words, there is always plenty of challenging and useful work to be done in cleaning up the mess that the geniuses leave behind them, while at the same time we owe them respect for their very real achievements. Indeed, a great deal of the task is deciding what these achievements really were and on what grounds they should be regarded as such. And it is in the course of this process of critical sorting out and evaluation that considerations gradually accumulate which eventually do lead either to the overthrow of older insights, or their incorporation into a new intellectual scheme, or perhaps more often, an uneasy combination of the two.

As its author conceived it, this little book was to be an effort along the second and more modest lines. I have not sought novelty or originality, qualities that at least in the study of human affairs seem to me rather overvalued. Nor do I flatter myself that my personal opinions have any significance as such. There may be opinions in the pages that follow that look personal in the sense of not being widely shared. There may even be some lines of thought that are novel. Neither aspect really matters. What does matter is the set of reasons offered in support of these views.

Documentation and the presentation of supporting evidence constitute problems in any such effort that seeks to be informal yet responsible. On this score I have borrowed a leaf from Veblen who asserted in the preface to his best known book that he would omit references on the grounds that the expert would recognize at once where his facts came from and that the general reader would not care. Since Veblen's solution does not seem to me altogether satisfactory, I have modified it from time to time in two ways. By my choice of wording I have tried to give the reader as clear a sense as possible of where he was treading familiar and presumably solid paths and where he might be gliding on very thin ice. Secondly, where it seemed to me that the reader had a special right to ask for the source of a particular assertion, a situation that arose most frequently in the last chapters on American society, I have tried to satisfy this need.

There are two final observations that I would like to make that derive from impressions the book has made upon its author in a stage close to its final form. (Incidentally most authors would, I suspect, agree that to a considerable extent any book "writes itself," even if the process can often demand very painful effort, because the author deals with topics that do have their own form and substance independent of his own thoughts, hopes, and wishes, even though this independence is never complete.) First, I am somewhat struck by how little I have had to say about what we loosely call personal unhappiness and misery, such as disappointment in love or other less intimate personal relations, while on the other hand I have always regarded such events as a major source of misery for the mass of humanity. There is nevertheless a reason for this apparent gap. Though some portion of personal unhappiness is probably an inevitable part of human fate, a very large portion is due to institutional causes. It is on these institutional causes, what can and cannot be done about them and at what probable costs, that the book focuses. Secondly, I have become aware that throughout the book there is an undercurrent of similarity between the stance that this book takes towards liberal institutions and that of at least some disaffected socialists towards the workings of Soviet society. This convergence includes even a certain sharing of ideals. For that I see no reason for apology. On the other hand, I would like to emphasize that the mere expression of anger is in my judgment light work, and that the analysis of causes and possible ways of affecting them rather more useful and significant.

For an author one of the most rewarding aspects of writing a book are the personal and intellectual debts incurred thereby. Over a period of some twenty years the delightful household of Herbert and Inge Marcuse has been a reserve home for my wife and me. There I have learned some of the art of asking embarrassing questions about human society. Gabriel and Joyce Kolko have tried, I hope successfully, to direct any such skill I may have acquired towards concrete issues in American society. In carefully criticizing a draft of this book they did their best to help me do justice to some views with which they disagree, an act of personal generosity and candor that was for me a very moving sign of commitment to shared intellectual ideals. Joint teaching with Robert Paul Wolff led to warm friendship with him and Cindy Wolff which increased and deepened my awareness of the distinction between plausible and correct arguments. It is not their fault if I have been unable to apply the distinction adequately to my own work.

Extended conversations with these and many other persons have left their mark all through the pages that follow. Among those that I recall with especial clarity and pleasure are several with Gar Alperovitz and with Albert O. Hirschman. Mr. Hirschman was kind enough to drop urgent tasks in order to check the degree of economic literacy in Chapter V. Naturally he bears no responsibility for solecisms that I may have added subsequently. This chapter also benefited from numerous discussions with two cohorts of lively students in a seminar on American society and foreign policy. Samuel Sharp's thoroughly detached and witty comments on all current political manifestations has been a source of refreshment that the accident of geography has prevented me from enjoying as often as I would have liked. Charles Nathanson has asked me many questions in a way that helped me to order my thoughts and also drew my attention to the literature on a pygmy society used in Chapter II.

To the Russian Research Center I am indebted for office space and the indispensable as well as unfailingly cheerful help of Rose Di Benedetto. In addition to typing the manuscript, she has struggled persistently and ingeniously to fend off chaos in a way for which my wife and I are grateful indeed. It would require another book to describe the ways in which Elizabeth Carol Moore has helped me. But if I could write it adequately, that would be for her eyes alone.

Portions of Chapters IV and VI have appeared in the *New York Review of Books* under the titles "On Rational Inquiry in Universities Today" (April 30, 1970) and "Revolution in America?" (January 30, 1969). Though both essays were written in response to immediate circumstances, I also intended them to be part of this book. As matters turned out I have used only a small part of the first essay and have considerably expanded the second one.

THE CAUSES OF HUMAN MISERY

I

On the Unity of Misery and
the Diversity of Happiness

For many centuries wise men and quite ordinary human beings have wondered about the meaning of happiness. Some have thought that genuine happiness was to be found only through the exercise of the higher powers of the intellect. Others, such as Freud, have maintained that artistic and intellectual pleasures were but pale imitations, if sometimes unavoidably necessary ones, of the genuine pleasures to be had from the satisfaction of physical drives and instincts. Some people find happiness through membership in a congenial community and the roles they are able to play in it; others detest community to seek contentment in solitude, contemplation, and privacy. Then there is the form of happiness that is generally considered abnormal, that to be had through making other people miserable. For an abnormal form of behavior it is enormously widespread: as soon as human beings manage to free themselves from the necessities of toil, they often display a subtle inventiveness in finding ways to make each other miserable, a form of behavior most obvious in the behavior of aristocracies towards their own members, but by no means confined to them. On the score of happiness, it is difficult to say anything more than that its sources seem infinitely various, and that disputes about tastes are notoriously hard to resolve.

Matters stand otherwise with misery and suffering, and the distinction will provide both a starting point for the reflections in this book and a recurring theme around which to order them. If human beings find it difficult to agree upon the meaning and causes of happiness, they find it much easier to know when they are miserable. Presumably it requires no laboriously accumulated proof to demonstrate that they have hardly ever really enjoyed 1) being tortured or slaughtered by a cruel enemy; 2) starvation and illness; 3) the exactions of ruthless authorities who carry off the fruits of prolonged labor; 4) the loss of beloved persons through the acts of others over which one has little or no control; 5) rotting in prison, being burned at the stake, or even simply losing the means of livelihood for the expression of heretical or unpopular beliefs. On this score too there are of course variations. Due to cultural and social conditioning some groups of people are better able to withstand suffering than others, and culturally sanctioned attitudes towards suffering vary considerably. Through ascetic practices human beings have deliberately taken upon themselves enormous amounts of misery. But they have done so in order to achieve some higher good or form of happiness. As the anthropologist Clyde Kluckhohn has pointed out, no known human culture has made of suffering an end in itself. Although this list is not a full catalogue of human miseries, it does cover a large segment of the range of human ills, probably their most severe forms. In any event it will give us more than enough to discuss.

In straightforward factual terms it is also possible to recognize certain widely recurring causes of human suffering. From the standpoint of social arrangements this time rather than from that of the individual human victim, and again in rough-and-ready empirical categories, these causes have been and remain 1) the ravages of war; 2) poverty, hunger, and disease; 3) injustice and oppression; and finally 4) persecution for dissident beliefs, a form of suffering, incidentally much more common in European societies than in Asiatic ones. The overwhelming mass of humanity has lived under these scourges for a very large portion of recorded history.

This conception of the unitary nature of human suffering, unitary at least in comparison with human happiness, is helpful in resolving some of the vexing issues of the proper role that subjective evaluations and moral judgments may or ought to play in social analysis.[1] The proper role of moral evaluation is one about

[1] Many social scientists hold that on this score they have fulfilled their obligation when they have stated their biases and inclinations plainly in a

which I am impertinent enough to believe that there exists much unnecessary confusion, though I am neither so arrogant nor so foolish as to anticipate widespread agreement upon the following observations.

In the past as in the present most serious issues have been simultaneously moral and political ones. They have concerned the way human society was to be organized; whether, for example, it was to be based on slavery or free labor, whether rewards were to go primarily to those with military capacities in the form of land as under feudalism, or to those with a talent for economic combinations as under capitalism, or in rarer cases to those with a combination of religious virtuosity and intellectual skills, as in the Indian caste system or theocratic societies. More abstractly, the questions that arouse human passions, especially in a time of change, have had to do with the forms of authority and justice, and the purposes of human life: that is, in what ways human beings were to be treated as means and as ends. From the beginning of recorded history all great changes have had behind them powerful currents of moral conviction about the ways in which human society ought and ought not to be organized, even though moral passions without material interests rarely if ever suffice to move large bodies of men and women in a way that leaves a deep mark upon the historical record. Moral issues, in other words, are necessarily what politics is about, though as we shall see in later chapters these two domains are not coextensive, and there appears to be an unavoidable conflict between them.

It is impossible therefore to avoid taking some kind of a moral position, not only in writing about politics but also in *not* writing about them and going about the ordinary business of daily life, as scholar, shoemaker, mechanic, or plumber. The refusal to be concerned with political issues is in itself a political stance, though not necessarily in favor of the status quo, as is frequently asserted. If the prevailing regime requires that the ordinary citizen give tangible evidence of correct political convictions, as is increasingly the

---

preface. Such statements, however, fail to meet the issues. Often they turn out to be varieties of ritual absolution or devices to propitiate a potential critic.

case in modern societies, the refusal of political concern, the with-drawal into private concerns, becomes an act of opposition, some-times even dangerous defiance. As for the student of human society, it is a truism that his conscious and unconscious moral assumptions and preferences will guide much of his work no mat-ter how objective he tries to be. At the very least, a scholar quite satisfied with the world in which he lives is unlikely to start out by asking the same questions as the one who feels a sense of outrage and nausea upon picking up the daily newspaper. On the other hand, neither complacency nor outrage is by itself an adequate guarantee that the investigator will ask correct questions, correct in the sense of leading to an accurate understanding of what takes place and why.

From these considerations it follows that moral judgments have not only an unavoidable but also a necessary and proper place in any attempt to make reasoned political judgments. But what moral judgments? Here is where the difficulties begin. There are many people today who apparently believe that once moral judgments enter a discussion, science necessarily flies out the window. Since, they agree, moral considerations are unavoidable, there can be no such thing as a scientific approach to human affairs. Moral judg-ments are inevitably arbitrary, this line of argument continues, and therefore no two people with different moral positions can possibly agree in their interpretation of social facts. This plea of *ignorabi-mus* seems to me both untenable and nihilistic.[2] Let me add right away, however, that I do not in the least wish to de-emphasize the

---

[2] Like many untenable ideas, it is in my judgment a misleading exaggera-tion of a valid insight, an awareness that social facts and moral evaluations of these facts can and do change over time. At one time, for example, slavery was regarded as something close to the natural order of the uni-verse, though Aristotle, who is often cited as holding this point of view, does, I think, betray a touch of uneasiness. (See Aristotle, *Politics*, I, ii, 13–15, in Loeb Classical Library edition, pp. 23, 25.) Later, for reasons that are ascertainable, though subject to continuing debate, slavery became for many people who were not slaves a morally reprehensible institution. That it was in some ways disagreeable at the very least for practically all slaves at all times seems reasonably clear, and constitutes one of the reasons for speaking of the unity of misery.

enormous difficulties in the way of reasoned agreement about matters that arouse political passion. The position to which I adhere sees the source of these obstacles in the frailties of human nature and the inadequacies of the evidence. On these grounds alone one may readily concede that perfect agreement is highly improbable or even impossible. That, however, is not the issue I am raising. What is at stake is whether the search for reasoned agreement is worthwhile because it is at least possible in principle (even if a goal we can never completely attain) or whether the enterprise is inherently an impossible one because all such judgments are necessarily arbitrary.

Political and historical judgments would be necessarily arbitrary, a matter of personal whim and preference, only if two conditions prevailed simultaneously. The first condition would be that moral preferences themselves were purely arbitrary, in the sense that there could exist no way of judging among them. Here the conception of the unitary nature of misery is helpful. It is, I believe, simply not the case that moral preferences are in fact purely arbitrary. The evidence is reasonably clear that human beings do not want a life of suffering, at least not for its own sake. Such evidence has led me to adopt as a working premise the moral position that human society ought to be organized in such a way as to eliminate useless suffering. I also very much want society to allow and indeed encourage human beings to find their own forms of happiness in their own ways so long as the search does not cause others to suffer. To be sure there is no strictly logical reason that I can perceive for adopting this standpoint. But are formal logical considerations the only ones, or by themselves the decisive ones, in reaching a decision that is in any case unavoidable?

That aspect of the issue may have stirred up more dust than is really necessary. If the factual evidence and the logic in a political treatise are sound, the moral starting point plays a very minor role towards the intellectual contribution that the treatise can make. One can reverse the moral premise without affecting the rest of the argument. In the case of this little book, if the general arguments are correct, presumably anyone who wished to increase human suffering would find the discussion pertinent.

The second condition is more complex. For political and historical judgments to be fundamentally a matter of personal preference and arbitrary whim it seems to me that there would have to be no real possibility of making correct and incorrect assertions about the facts or causal connections among the facts.[3] Highly respected thinkers have taken this negative position, which, as far as I can ascertain, has modern roots in both Hume and Kant. In writings about history and politics we usually find it in a somewhat more eclectic form. A certain substratum of facts, such as Napoleon's loss of the battle of Waterloo in the year 1815, is taken as established beyond dispute. But their meaning, significance, and relationship to each other, are somehow the product of the human observer.

Now it is quite true that the notion of knowledge makes no sense without someone to do the knowing. Thus knowledge implies some form of interaction between observer and observed, an interaction that does take on some special characteristics when human beings observe other human beings, an aspect to be discussed shortly. It is also quite true that observation is always guided by preconceptions, ways of ordering the data, that vary greatly from individual to individual and even more from one cultural epoch to another.[4] But neither point tells us anything about the correctness of the knowledge. For knowledge to be correct, it seems to me that the assertions have to represent correctly the relationships that exist in and among the facts. Essentially for this reason I find myself quite unable to accept this negative position and hold that the second condition for an *inevitably* arbitrary or perspectivist view of human affairs cannot be fulfilled.

The facts of human society and the causal connections among them, to put the point positively, are real in the quite ordinary

[3] The concept of cause, I am aware, is somewhat suspect in advanced epistemological circles. Nevertheless I find it indispensable and will continue to use it in the sense of a determinate and discoverable connection among two or more facts. Facts themselves of course display varying degrees of complexity.

[4] E. H. Gombrich's conception of schema and correction takes account of this relationship. See his *Art and Illusion* (Princeton, 1960; London, 1962), the work of a luminous and cultivated intelligence that sheds light far beyond its immediate subject matter.

commonsense meaning of the word. They have an existence and structure quite independent of the observer who tries to understand them, whether this observer is conservative, liberal, or radical. The moral preferences of the observer have nothing to do with the existence of these facts or their inherent, objective structure and relationship to each other. An observer who wittingly or unwittingly allows himself to substitute these preferences for reality simply deceives himself and others. One who does so deliberately is plainly dishonest, though that is relatively rare.

What the position I have argued amounts to is a stress on the familiar point that causal analysis and evaluation are distinct if related activities. Both seem to me unavoidable, and some of the main difficulties arise from the fact that it is often necessary to carry on both simultaneously. The legitimate role of moral concern is to lend salience or relevance to some facts and to put others in the background. In the old-fashioned cinema melodrama, the fact that the heroine is tied to the railroad tracks a mile or so in front of an onrushing train, is very relevant to the hero galloping to the crucial spot with a knife between his teeth. By empathy it is also relevant to the audience. Other facts, such as the number of stones between each railroad tie, are not relevant to the hero. They might of course be very relevant to a track maintenance engineer inspecting the tracks to see if they need repairs. But what we look for in the facts does not change the facts; it is only a first step towards changing them. Their structure is the same no matter what we are looking for. The significance is quite literally *in* the facts.

Quite often the significance can be in the facts themselves quite unknown to observers and participants. If the horse on which the hero is galloping stumbles and falls on a small boulder in the path, the hero will make a very unpleasant discovery about the significance of this fact. If his laudable moral desires to rescue the heroine as fast as possible leads him to pay no attention to the state of the ground over which he is galloping, the hero is all the more likely to come to grief in this fashion.

In the simple affairs of daily life, not artificial melodramas, most human beings do not need to be told in abstract terms that allowing moral preferences or hopes and fears to cloud their judgment can have disastrous results. They learn this for themselves. Unfortunately those who write about politics and society, as well as those who act in this arena, often face no such direct penalty for the failure to realize where morality begins and ends. Instead, other innocent people often pay the extreme penalty for the self-deception of their intellectual and political leaders.

Nevertheless the little melodrama with the heroine still tied to the railroad tracks will be useful in clarifying certain further issues, the distinctive nature of social facts, their resistance to change, and the costs of changing them. The hero of the melodrama is extraordinarily anxious to change the fact that the heroine is bound to the railroad tracks by stout cords, presumably tied by a villain with a dark moustache at some previous time. With his sharp knife between his teeth the hero has the means to alter this fact at very little cost to himself, no more, let us say, than making his trusty horse rather sweaty and lame.

It would be pleasant if the problems of real life were that simple. The melodrama brings out a simple point frequently made and perhaps even more often forgotten: social facts are the product of human action. They are in this sense artifacts. Therefore one of the most important things for the social analyst to find out is why they are facts at all. Who tied the heroine to the tracks and why? In this instance as well as those in real life an important part of the answer is that some identifiable and concrete human individuals make equally concrete gains from the facts being what they are, while other human beings lose out for the same reason. That is why social investigation so often has a political cutting edge.

At the same time it is important to remember that in pointing out the political implications of an argument one has said nothing whatsoever about the validity of the argument. It is a common polemical device to discredit a line of argument by demonstrating that it leads to unwanted political conclusions, to conservative conclusions if the polemicist is addressing a radical audience and vice versa. Though the attempt may be useful in provoking further thought and a reexamination of the issues, even if the demonstration is flawless it really proves nothing about the issues under debate.

That, it seems to me, is the fundamental reason why one has to let the political chips fall where they will in serious social analysis. There is no innate guarantee that valid social analysis will always yield conclusions favorable to the humanitarian impulse.[5] About all that one can say on this score with any assurance is rather obvious. On any specific problem only one set of arguments can of course be valid. Valid arguments that point to the difficulties and obstacles in changing human institutions have conservative to reactionary implications. Those that indicate ways of overcoming these difficulties with varying degrees of ease have liberal to radical implications.

It is often pointed out that a radical—here as elsewhere in the sense of leftist radical—faces a peculiarly difficult intellectual task because it is impossible in advance to prove that a new and as yet untried social order is really a viable one. The most radicals can hope to demonstrate with factual evidence is that the potential for better arrangements already exists in the form of, let us say, an advanced technology, a high level of education, and the like. On the other hand, the reactionary at the opposite end of the spectrum cannot really hope to prove that what exists must necessarily continue to exist. Nor can the liberal demonstrate that incremental and gradual change will always work. The facts are the same for all, right across the political spectrum, and the epistemological difficulties seem just about equal. Some facts, notably those of past history, are completely beyond anyone's power to change. Naturally, our *knowledge* of these facts changes continually. All that it is possible to do is to alter the consequences. In some instances the change may cost so much as to be virtually out of the question. In others they may be well within the range of conceivable concerted

---

[5] I used to think that there might be some general drift in that direction because the dominant groups in any society are generally the ones who have more to hide about the way the society works. Hence critical exposure would generally favor the Left. Further investigation into the character of lower-class oppositional and revolutionary movements has made me more aware that they too have a great deal to hide (and to exaggerate) for their own political reasons. On that account I have become skeptical of any such drift.

human effort. That is a matter for concrete investigation from
case to case.

With the proviso that it is always necessary to ask *cost for
whom*, the conception of varying costs provides a useful way of
getting around the philosophical bogs of determinism versus in-
determinism. Instead of asking whether or not a particular social
arrangement or practice (such as, for example, war) is somehow
inevitable or determined, one tries to ascertain the conditions under
which it does and does not occur. If one opposes the practice, one
tries to learn from these conditions something about the probable
costs and benefits of changing matters, and what the prospects
for getting support for this change are. Thus in somewhat sche-
matic form the sequence goes from moral concern through causal
analysis to political action. In real life of course these three processes are as a rule going on simultaneously and reacting back and
forth on each other.

On grounds that are quite justified some readers may react very
negatively to the very words cost and benefit. They have a Penta-
gonese odor which suggests the prospect of some technocratic elite
based on slide rules and computers in the hands of an arrogant set
of social scientists. Though the association is an unfortunate historical fact, I shall not for that reason avoid using these terms from
time to time. Because those who contribute to human misery may
use some limited forms of reasoned discourse constitutes no ground
for the abandonment of reason. After all, there is nothing else as a
way of discovering truth or acting rationally. There is an even
more important reason for sticking to the notion of costs and benefits: it cannot, in my judgment, lead to the supremacy of a technological elite. To be sure, some sort of technocratic absolutism
might arise for other reasons. But it would have to be based on
pseudo-science with wildly exaggerated claims—claims that a
proper scientific attitude would rapidly explode. As we shall see in
due course at various points in this book, there are powerful reasons for holding that in facing some of the most crucial issues the
area of uncertainty is bound to remain painfully large. Those who
fear the prospect of a technocratic absolutism are not to be dis-

legacy to future definitions of friend and foe, just as Hebrew, Greek, and Christian traditions bequeathed some notions that became part of liberal and socialist thought.

There are then some broad constants in the problem of human misery and, certainly of equal and perhaps greater importance, ascertainable historical trends that affect both the specific historical form of these constants and human efforts to cope with them. Hence the main task becomes one of trying to assess the underlying currents of social change, their direction and power, *together with* the human costs of any effort to change their direction and that of refusing to make such an effort. As pointed out earlier, this viewpoint is neither determinist nor anti-determinist, a distinction that is too gross to be helpful if it is valid at all. Only if it is possible to get some sense of the probable obstacles and costs in human suffering, as well as the possible benefits from present and future policies, a sense that can never be more than a rough approximation, can we avoid succumbing to the defeatist illusion of impotence within a permanent present or the opposite one of romantic utopianism. Since these two illusions themselves have been among the major sources of human misery, the effort to overcome them remains worthwhile. It is indeed the central justification for the role of detached observer of human affairs.

II

Of War, Cruelty, Oppression, and General Human Nastiness

The Latin tag, *homo homini lupus*, we have recently been told, is a slander on the wolf. Among living beings, humans are evidently quite extraordinary for the amount of cruel violence they inflict upon members of their own species. The most obvious form of human violence is war, with which we may as well begin. Of all known human societies only a handful of those without a written language have had no experience of the excitement and ravages of war.[1] For many a society, military institutions present an excellent starting point for the analysis and understanding of the society as a whole, often a better starting point than the analysis of economic arrangements. Military obligations and military organization strongly influenced class relationships and politics in both Greek and Roman society. The essence of feudal society was the grant of land in return for military service. Religion, law, morality, the character of the social bonds that hold a society together are often traceable to warfare. The upper classes in all literate societies control, at least during periods of law and order and social stability,

[1] About one such society, the Tongas, who inhabit a tiny speck on the map of the Pacific, we are fortunate enough to have a record of the introduction of warfare and how the Tongans enthusiastically used the new activity to relieve periods of inaction and boredom. See John Martin, *An Account of the Natives of the Tonga Islands, in the South Pacific Ocean*, 3rd edition (Edinburgh, 1827), Vol. I, 77–79. In assessing their pleasure it is necessary to remember that warfare in non-literate societies is generally, though not always, much less of a blood-thirsty and absorbing activity than among "civilized" societies.

the means of violence and coercion against other societies, as well as against threats of internal disorder. The moral justifications for their superiority in any given case uphold their monopoly of internal and external violence, a monopoly that is of course often short of absolute. In turn these justifications, the bases of their legitimacy and authority, give the upper classes the right to extract an economic surplus from the underlying population, a surplus that they turn into what we loosely call civilization. In this manner warfare becomes an integral part of peace and the social order.

Although war and its consequences are a nearly universal aspect of human experience, this aspect is an enormously varied one. At one end of the range of known variations there have been highly warlike societies. At the other end, there have been a few completely peaceful ones in remote corners of the earth. Furthermore, behavior within the same society changes over time: the supposedly aggressive Japanese sealed themselves up in their own islands between 1603 and 1868, during which time their military class eventually came to suffer from severe structural unemployment. Even in warlike societies it is necessary to resort to a wide variety of sanctions and inducements to persuade people to fight. The draft is scarcely the most popular institution in any modern country. These facts cast severe doubt on the thesis that the desire to kill and destroy other human beings is part of the innate and nearly constant biological equipment of the human species.

Here we reach the vexed question of whether aggression is an instinct. On this score a great deal depends on what we mean by instinct. If we adopt a strict definition, it is quite clear that aggression is not an instinct. By a strict definition we mean that an instinct is some sort of biological drive towards a specific form of behavior, in this case killing or severely injuring other human beings, that the organism cannot resist or without whose satisfaction the species ceases to exist. Without food, water, and sleep the human organism will perish in a short period of time. The drives behind these needs we can call instincts in the quite narrow sense. Sex belongs in a somewhat more puzzling category. The human organism does not perish without sexual satisfaction, though the demand for its satisfaction is very powerful at frequently recurring intervals. If there were clearly attested cases of human individuals living out their entire life span without any form of sexual satisfaction, i.e. without even masturbation or homosexual experiences, we might have grounds for refusing to label the sexual drive as an instinct. On the other hand, no isolated human society can maintain itself without heterosexual relationships. Therefore it appears best to label the sexual drive as an instinct in the narrow sense.

For an instinct thus narrowly defined, it is sufficient to demonstrate the existence of one negative case in order to prove that it is not an instinct. Shortly there will be occasion to discuss some of this negative evidence. In any event it is already clear that human aggressive tendencies are quite different from the instincts just discussed. For that reason it will be better to consider aggression as one of many human capacities, rather than as an instinct. It is a capacity that only too obviously can be made to surface in actual behavior under a huge variety of historical and social circumstances. Nevertheless under this conception the issue changes its character. The evidence enables us to reject any variant of pessimistic conservatism based on biologically determined human nature. Other considerations, as we shall see in due course, *may* force us back to a pessimistic prognosis. But at this point the evidence indicates a different line of questioning. Clearly social institutions play an enormous role in both encouraging and discouraging aggressive behavior. Whatever human capacity or tendency there may be in this direction is evidently sufficiently plastic and modifiable to make its expression relatively harmless over extended periods of time and under appropriate conditions.

What are the appropriate conditions? Is there any prospect of putting them into effect in any foreseeable future and on a wider scale? It is possible to gain considerable insight into these issues by examining two sets of data, those about non-literate societies where war is unknown and the situations of modern states that have enjoyed peace for long periods of time. In neither case are the inferences reassuring.

The Mbuti, central African pygmies, constitute an excellent example of what I have elsewhere called a decent society, that is, one without war, oppression, or physical suffering.[2] The key to their good fortune lies in their relation to the enormous tropical rain forest in which they live, and through the forest to their neighbors, Negro villagers who live by farming in clearings on the edge of the forest. These cultivators attempt rather unsuccessfully to exploit the pygmies as agricultural laborers. Since the pygmies know how to live in the forest and the villagers do not, the pygmies can abscond to the forest whenever they feel so inclined. Thus the pygmies are able to treat their village "masters" with mock deference. By working for them rather slackly and amiably cheating them, the pygmies obtain certain food and whatever small articles they need. The villagers regard the forest as an hostile place, whose desirable products the pygmies supply (meat and honey, as well as saplings and leaves for building houses). By fleeing into the forest at their own convenience the pygmies can be safe and independent without resorting to armed self-defense. As white civilization has encroached on the area, the situation has changed somewhat, affecting the villagers more than the pygmies. The Belgian administrators have siphoned off young males in the villages to use for road construction and have instituted the growing of new commercial crops, like cotton, for which the villagers need an increased labor force at harvest time. With their own men away, the villagers have become more dependent than ever on their "wayward servants," the pygmies, who seem to remain as independent as ever.[3]

The enormous forests provide the pygmies with a cool, healthy environment, materials for adequate shelter, and enough to eat, in contrast with the burning sun, oppressive dust, and filthy water of the villages, an environment in which pygmies evidently suffer as much as white anthropologists. In the forest the pygmies live in small bands, loosely organized around the task of hunting, in which various age groups have distinct but complementary jobs to perform. There are plenty of signs of aggression and ordinary human nasti-

[2] What follows is based on Colin M. Turnbull, *The Forest People* (New York, 1961), and his *Wayward Servants: The Two Worlds of the African Pygmies* (New York, 1965; London, 1966).

[3] Turnbull, *Wayward Servants*, 39–40.

ness in the form of matrimonial quarrels and disputes over the distribution of food when the hunt has been successful, which it evidently is most of the time. Relatively mild group sanctions such as ridicule or the threat of ostracism, which is never carried out—to do so would be a real death sentence—are enough to keep this aggression under control. Though Turnbull does not say so explicitly, it looks as though the imperatives of working together on the hunt, a cooperation that does at times seem close to collapsing, are barely sufficient to damp down socially dangerous aggression.

Indeed, one of the more curious and attractive features of Mbuti pygmy society is that they have just about as many social rules as they need and no more. Even if one allows for a touch of romanticism in Turnbull's account, the pygmies have a singularly unoppressive culture. They have made for themselves no oppressive taboos and have about as light-hearted an attitude towards their own social regulations as it seems possible to have and still maintain the degree of social cohesion necessary for their particular form of society. They have neither chiefs nor an organized priesthood, nor of course any warriors. They derive a deep emotional pleasure from their ceremonials, yet have a completely matter-of-fact attitude towards the instruments of ceremony.[4]

How and why the Mbuti developed this light-hearted, pragmatic, yet far from Philistine attitude towards their own culture is impossible to ascertain, though this outlook must be at least partly connected with the simple requirements of living in small bands of roving hunters and gatherers. Whatever the reason, it is clear that these pygmies have managed to create a society largely free from external and internal oppression. Though aggression is certainly present among the pygmies, it is mild enough to dispose of any theory to the effect that where hostile feelings find no outlet

[4] The ceremonies require the use of a musical instrument that plays a central role in this culture. It was originally made with much labor by hollowing out the trunk of a tree. The instrument, whose existence theoretically must be kept secret from the women (although the women know all about it), used to rot rapidly when kept in its hiding place. Now they use an old piece of rusty iron pipe because it lasts much longer. This trait expresses the mood of the whole culture.

against an external enemy they will discharge themselves in the form of cruelty towards members of the same society.

In the anthropological literature there is a scattering of other cases of societies without war, oppression, and other forms of socially created misery. It is worth noticing that certain Eskimos, whose physical environment is in terms of temperature and raw physical comfort the exact opposite of the pygmies' forest, also lack war, hereditary class divisions, and other paraphernalia of oppression. The basic reasons are apparently similar: a physical environment to which they have worked out an effective adaptation and which until very recently no one else wanted, plenty of space for their own small bands organized around a form of subsistence, hunting, that requires a division of labor without marked or permanent hierarchical traits. There are indications, however, that the Eskimos' way of life generates much more anger than the pygmies' and that the Eskimos' social mechanisms for controlling this anger are not very effective.[5] Further examples of non-literate societies without war either depend upon isolation from potential enemies or else involve complete capitulation to an enemy.[6]

Thus the Mbuti pygmies present us with a paradigm example of a peaceful and unoppressive society. They have apparently created a world of their own, quite similar to that found in the hopes and dreams of the communitarian and neo-anarchist current in Western radicalism, an ancient and powerful current that has surfaced again prominently in the New Left, partly in reaction to the political success and moral decomposition of authoritarian Marxism and Western liberalism. For twentieth-century radicalism, however, the implications of the pygmies' achievement are, as far as I can see, strictly negative, because the conditions that made that achievement possible are impossible to reproduce now. Even among non-literate societies these favorable conditions were very unusual. For no

[5] See E. A. Hoebel, *The Law of Primitive Man* (Cambridge, Mass., 1961), 82–90.

[6] See M. R. Davie, *The Evolution of War: A Study of Its Role in Early Societies* (New Haven, 1929; London, 1968), Chap. IV for an early attempt to collect the major instances. I have been unable to locate any more recent effort.

modern society can there now be the equivalent of the tropical forest to shelter it from potentially predatory neighbors. There is hardly any likelihood that modern men and women would be able and willing to stabilize their demands upon their physical environment in such a way as to leave a surplus for all, and above all a surplus of space in which to roam with a light burden of cultural and physical obligations. Given the size of the world's population there is no serious prospect that human beings can organize themselves into small autonomous groups largely isolated from each other. The catastrophic cultural impoverishment that would follow such a destruction of the division of labor is a contingency few are likely to find acceptable, no matter how negative their attitude towards contemporary civilization. If isolation, space, simple technology and living in small bands are the only hope for a peaceful and happy world, then one can merely repeat that the message for civilized man is: leave all hope behind. . . .

The conclusions to be drawn from modern examples of peaceful states, such as Switzerland and Sweden, or of prolonged peaceful relationships between two adjacent states, as in the often cited instance of the United States and Canada, are scarcely more reassuring. Three sets of circumstances, either singly or in combination, will account for these apparent exceptions to the generalization that the normal relationships among sovereign and independent human societies is one of war or preparation for war. All the examples mentioned concern the fate of weak states in the context of intermittent wars among much more powerful states. In this general context a powerful state may be able to exercise all the control it needs or wants over a weaker neighbor without the trouble and bloodshed of territorial conquest. (There is quite a bit of evidence to indicate that this is the case in American relations with Canada.) In some instances, to be sure, this degree of control may be rather slight because the interests of the two countries as determined by the larger context of international conflicts create few seriously divisive issues. This situation shades off into the second one where a small or weak country finds itself in a back eddy of international politics. In this situation two or more hostile powers develop stand-off relationships in parts of the world. Great power statesmen in these instances again prefer the neutrality and independence of the weak power to the risks and dangers of conquering it. Finally, a small state can within limits increase its freedom to maneuver in the back eddies of world politics by increasing its own military strength to a degree that makes outright conquest a less and less palatable prospect for the strategists of a great power. This is the well-known bee-sting strategy of the weak. Though the sting may be relatively harmless and even kill the bee, it is sufficiently disagreeable to deter human beings from attacking bees.

In all of these cases the weak state owes its peace and independence to the conflict among the more powerful. Though statesmen and intellectual leaders in the weaker states may express sentiments of moral superiority and mild outrage over the bellicose behavior of the larger states,[7] their moral superiority is actually parasitic upon the violence that they condemn. That seems to be true of the more attractive moralities in general. The peaceful situation of the weaker and peaceful states exists on the sufferance of the strong and more bellicose ones: the happiness of the former depends upon the simple fact that aggression against them is not worthwhile.

Worthwhile for whom? And in what sense worthwhile? If there is no instinct behind the whole process, why is it that human beings treat killing one another as a thoroughly worthwhile activity, often devoting their best treasure, brains, and inventive skills in social organization to this end?

An answer couched in terms of material interests alone is obviously inadequate. In the first place, material interests change historically. A hunting tribe has a different set of material interests from a community based on agriculture, and both will differ from societies based on slavery, commerce, or manufacturing. In this sense what is worth fighting for at one stage of historical development may have no value at another. Coal in the Pennsylvania hills was of no importance to the Indians who inhabited this territory; it became significant for the white man at a certain stage of tech-

[7] Even De Gaulle, for all his alleged realism, has expressed himself in this tone, a reflection of France's actual situation. More numerous instances can be found in the public expression of Swiss, Swedish, Indian, and Canadian spokesmen.

nology and may cease to be significant at another. Societies may of course come into armed conflict with each other even when their material interests in a piece of territory are very different: witness the struggles between American Indians trying to preserve their hunting grounds and the white settlers who encroached as subsistence and later as commercial farmers. To the extent that technological changes create new material interests, while the old ones persist or die out rather slowly, one can anticipate an increase in the causes of war.

Even when corrected through the introduction of an historical perspective, the notion of material interests as somehow basic to any explanation of social conflict remains in my judgment misleading. Moral conflicts, that is conflicts over moral principles, are not necessarily always reducible to conflicts among material interests, though they often have an obvious connection with such interests. Indeed it is the moral conflict between principles of social organization that puts passion behind material interests and makes these material interests appear to be irreconcilable.[8]

This relationship requires closer examination. In any given society at any moment in time the historian or contemporary observer can perceive the struggle to create and sustain what we can call, as a tentative first approximation, a specific moral identity. We can detect echoes of this struggle in Aeschylus's dramatic reconstruction of the Persian wars and the glorification of Athenian democracy that Thucydides put into the mouth of Pericles. It is a struggle that particular identifiable[9] groups of human beings have waged simultaneously against their physical environment, against other groups in their own society, and against other societies. Hegel noticed this human tendency to create an identity through conflict with others and erected it into a general philosophical principle. Identity is, however, rather too abstract a term, though the identification with each other that human beings create in this fashion is an important consequence. What they do create are the

[8] Hence in the more important historical conflicts the two elements become inseparable, all the more so as material means are necessary to accomplish moral ends.

[9] Where the evidence survives. Is Lethe or Clio the muse of History?

stable yet historically changing patterns of cooperation and hostility: social institutions, mores, folkways, cultural patterns, etc. As part of this process, and in ways that Freud opened to our understanding (especially through his conception of the superego), human beings create and acquire moral principles. These principles contain an explanation of human suffering and indicate the limits of what humanity can do about its miseries. The same principles by which we learn to distinguish friend from foe are the main supports of the social order.

At this point, however, social order itself becomes a deceptive abstraction. Except perhaps in very small and simple societies, principles of legitimacy are the principles 1) of the groups that dominate the society, that exercise authority in the society; 2) of those who seek to dominate the society, who challenge the prevailing principles, who endeavor to create not justifications for authority but standards by which to condemn that authority; 3) of those who seek primarily to escape from the demands of the prevailing order, to justify a refusal of allegiance, or at least of total allegiance ("Render unto Caesar" . . . but also . . . "Give up all that thou hast and follow me").

The relative importance of each of these choices and themes varies enormously in time and place. To be effective, revolutionary challenges in the sense of articulate and theoretically argued standards of condemnation, must be combined with an effort to create and harness the popular sentiments necessary in order to bring about major political and economic changes. Revolution seems to be a relatively recent and distinctly Western cultural invention, appearing in full bloom for the first time with the French Revolution. On the other hand, Western history has, from the very beginning, been a conflict between opposing principles of social organization: from the age of the struggle between the Persian bureaucratic monarchy and the Greek city state through that between paganism and organized Christianity, down to the rise of modern social forms out of and against feudalism and royal absolutism. This struggle of course continues in our own time, now mainly between advanced industrial capitalism and efforts at revolutionary modernization.

There has been, we can perhaps now perceive, an explicit social purpose behind these massive slaughters, tortures, cruelties, behind the desolation, disease, and starvation that have strewn the record of human history. But it is not a purpose in the older semi-theological sense of leading up to a final liberation from misery. More exactly, there have been different and opposing objectives pursued by different groups. There appears to have been some group purpose behind nearly all cruelty ranging from the grisly initiation rites and punishments among pre-literate groups, to the tortures and brutalities of the Nazi concentration camps, as well as the horrors of our own day. Some aspects of human cruelty are historically specific, that is, they are the consequences of the struggle to establish or prevent the establishment of historically specific institutions such as Christianity, feudalism, capitalism, liberal democracy, socialism. Other aspects are more readily comprehensible in terms of general and recurring sociological causes that are independent of specific historical configurations and epochs. The general role of cruelty, then, is to sustain or to subvert and overthrow a specific social order. There is very little cruelty in the human record that one can identify as random or purposeless or primarily for the pleasure to be derived from watching the victims suffer.

This observation does not mean that the pleasure does not exist. It is obvious that there is such a pleasure, or that such a pleasure can be an only too easily acquired taste. However, it is also worth noticing that in many such instances—for example, in the cases of lynch mobs or fascist guards beating and bullying concentration camp prisoners—the perpetrators of cruelty define the victim as in some way non-human or not quite human.[10] There is a risk or fear of pollution in these situations, clearly tied to the preservation of a specific social order.[11] The same is true of revolutionaries, as appears very clearly in the symbolism of the French Revolution as well as the Puritan Revolution

[10] See Winthrop D. Jordan, *White Over Black* (Pelican Books, 1969), 183–184, 233–234.

[11] Cf. Mary Douglas, "Pollution," *International Encyclopedia of the Social Sciences* (New York, 1968), 336–342.

that preceded it and the communist ones that followed it. On both sides of the barricades "our" social order is the "pure" one threatened by contamination from its opponents. Even the murder of a completely innocent victim is often the acting out of defiance and contempt for the prevailing conventional morality. Indeed, it is precisely this defiance which produces the reaction of horror among respectable citizens. Socially respectable forms of cruelty that support the established order and its beneficiaries—executions, imprisonments, war—generally arouse much less of a shudder.

It is this intimate connection between cruelty and the struggles to maintain or change an historically specific social order that make cruelty very difficult to define. It also provides a reason for waiting to clarify this point until we are well into the subject matter. Cruelty turns out to be mainly the infliction of pain and suffering for a purpose. Our negative moral judgment has to do not only with the pain but also with the purpose. A surgeon may inflict a great deal of pain on a patient. Educated people today do not regard the surgeon as cruel so long as he uses the best knowledge available to make the patient suffer less in the long run than the patient otherwise could be expected to suffer from his disease or injury. The patient is unable to judge the surgeon's skill except in a very rough fashion by reputation and results.

From this commonplace example we can see that the conception of cruelty requires factual judgments about 1) the purpose of the suffering, 2) the knowledge and competence of the person imposing it, and 3) the length of time involved. An act is not considered cruel if after the passage of a certain period of time either the victim or some other people undergo less suffering.

Of these three contextual elements that of time presents the most difficult problems. How much suffering do revolutionaries have a right to impose upon the present generation for the sake of the happiness of future generations? As Lenin asked, by what yardstick can one measure the amount of repression necessary for the victory of a revolution? Though the answer is inherently uncertain, to deny that a criterion can exist at all removes all possible limits on arbitrary cruelty. Not even the worst dictator goes that far. He has to retain the support of at least some followers. Since such judgments occur, and, to repeat, are unavoidable because the decision *not* to make a revolution *also* has consequences for present and future suffering, there must be better and worse ways of making them.

Two closely connected considerations evidently enter into any such judgment. The first is the length of time it will be necessary to wait or suffer for the benefits to materialize. Obviously the longer this time period the greater the discount any reasonable person will place on promises of such benefits. It is also clear that perspectives on such promises will also differ in accord with degrees of present misery, and thus at least roughly along class lines. The second consideration has to do with the certainty of the benefits to be derived, and is thus related to the competence of the authority (or anti-authority) who imposes the suffering. The less the certainty, which of course increases with the length of time it is necessary to suffer or wait, the less justification there is for the suffering. Since complete certainty is impossible and a decision is unavoidable, this decision would have to be based on the best knowledge available at the time, i.e. for that specific historical period.

Though this attempt to clarify the meaning of cruelty may seem abstract and to some readers even banal, applying it leads to results that at least for this author are surprising and disagreeable. For example, by this reasoning the agent of the Inquisition, to the extent that he acted in accord with the best knowledge of his day, turns out to have not been cruel. His victims we may be sure had quite different feelings. There is no reason to ignore their feelings. Pain is a very objective matter. The point is merely once more that by itself the infliction of pain is not necessarily cruel, though the failure to minimize pain where that is possible is indeed cruel. What is unavoidable pain in an earlier historical epoch can become deliberate cruelty if it is allowed to continue in a later one. The reason the Inquisitor's cruelty seems so ghastly to modern educated people is that most of us no longer believe in eternal damnation and eternal bliss. If there really were such things as eternal damnation and eternal bliss from which the human soul could be saved, the torturers of the Inquisition could justify their acts by asserting that the relatively brief suffering they imposed helped to save the soul of the victim (in cases of recantation, where the situation is analogous to that of the surgeon) and by deterring others from theological error. Similarly, the reason why educated people today have supported either revolutionary terror or the horrors of the war in Vietnam is at least partly due to a belief in factual evidence for the assertion that one or the other has played, or can play, a part in creating or preserving a social order that is by some criterion superior to its opposing form. Even a person who abhors violence on principle cannot avoid making this kind of judgment. If he refuses to use violence against a cruel oppressor, to make political sense such a refusal has to be based on an empirical judgment that the result will be less cruelty for humanity as a whole or some segment of it.[12]

Finally, it is necessary to stress that the social and political reasons for imposing pain and suffering always have to be made on an inadequate basis. The inadequacy applies equally to the act and the refusal to act, both of which contain unknown consequences for the future as well as the prospect of unknown criteria for judging these consequences. The agent of the Inquisition could not possibly anticipate the rise of the secular outlook that would utterly destroy all justification for his acts. Today we cannot possibly anticipate the moral standards of human society a few centuries ahead, or even if there will be such a thing as human society. All that we can do, and that indeed is considerable, is to try to improve in every possible way the factual and theoretical bases for unavoidable decisions. The calm confidence—or ecstasy—of the political leader who sends masses of humanity to their death for the sake of a shining distant future is indeed abominable. Equally abominable is the complacency of those liberals willing to rain terror from the skies while they prate about the virtues of pragmatic gradualism.

[12] The refusal may also of course and often is based on a personal refusal to engage in acts felt to be immoral in themselves, no matter what the social and political consequences are. Since the consequences are unavoidable, these acts do not make political sense, even though they may, as Weber pointed out, deserve deep respect on some other grounds.

Repulsive moral certainty is not limited to fanatics, while the refusal to act in clear circumstances where the consequences are apparent can have its own tragic results.

To assert that revolutionary and lesser forms of violence have played a very important role in bringing about what degrees of freedom and even of happiness a considerable sector of humanity now enjoys does not imply that violence was an unavoidable historical necessity in the past. The Revolt of the Netherlands, the Puritan Revolution, the French Revolution, and the American Civil War did help to break down in each case a different historical set of institutional obstacles to the establishment of Western liberal democracy, though it is of course impossible to prove that they were necessary to bring about this result. From the standpoint of a general commitment against human suffering there is nothing attractive about violence *per se*. Nor does the limited degree of "success" in past violence prove that present and future violence is good, inevitable, and necessary. Is it possible, therefore, to specify some of the conditions under which a resort to violence is justifiable? Though human beings do not generally make such decisions in a calm mood of rational calculation, this fact does not mean that objective conditions may not exist.

Although there is a very great element of inherent uncertainty in such judgments, I want to suggest that certain ones are indeed possible, as well as to indicate some of the intellectual difficulties in reaching them. We can begin with two of the less difficult types of situation that provide justification for the violent resistance to established authority. One is self-defense against the arbitrary abuse of authority. Another is to compel those in authority to listen to legitimate grievances (legitimate in this context meaning grievances whose removal would indeed reduce human suffering) and to act upon them. Even in these instances there are nevertheless difficulties. It is simply not true that the violence of the oppressed is *always* justified, because their violence may under certain circumstances merely make matters worse for everybody, themselves included. One of the most agonizing cases is that of violent resistance to tyranny without any prospect of success, such as the rising in

the Warsaw ghetto against the Nazis.[13] Does the leader of such
an uprising have the moral right to expose those with less courage
to certain death by reprisals? Will the gesture serve as sufficient
inspiration to encourage others to undertake more effective resistance? In advance there can be, as far as I can see, no answers to
such questions.

The third justification is to remove and destroy institutional
obstacles to a social order that will cause less suffering—that of
revolution, the most violent and uncertain of the three. To make
such a judgment it would be necessary to balance the horrors and
suffering caused by allowing the continuing regime to continue
against those of the revolution itself. Certainly one cannot know
the outcome for certain in advance. Nevertheless it does seem to
me possible to make some rough distinctions for which empirical
evidence is conceivable. There is a huge difference between the
violence that occurs in the course of efforts to sweep aside the
stubborn remnants of an *ancien régime* that has outlived its time,
and that the mass of the population has come to reject, and the
kind of violence required to sustain an "educational dictatorship"
in order to create a new and "better" variety of human beings and
social arrangements. The first situation, incidentally, appears to
have been mainly the one that Marx had in mind, while the second
is rather clearly what Stalin was trying to accomplish. The time
element in such judgments provides the greatest difficulties. When
de Tocqueville wrote about the French Revolution, he could present a reasonable case to the effect that the change had not been
worth the cost in human suffering; a century later we can see the
situation differently and have at least some grounds for concluding
that without the French Revolution French history might well
have taken a turn in the general direction of fascism. A hundred
years hence there might be similar arguments about the Bolshevik
Revolution and even Stalinism. Furthermore, the victims of suffering are bound to have a different perspective from those who
benefit therefrom. About all one can say on this score, borrowing

[13] See Michel Borwicz, *L'Insurrection du ghetto de Varsovie* (Paris,
1966).

a leaf from the economists, is that future and uncertain benefits require a heavy discount in any attempt at rational calculation.

Finally, it is necessary to notice that the failure of revolutionary violence, perhaps even the failure to exert sufficient violence in crucial circumstances when huge alternatives hang in the balance, may lead to tragic results that last for generations. German history is especially suggestive in considering this issue, though there is always room for debate about what the underlying tendencies actually were and what prospects actually existed for the success of a more vigorously revolutionary policy.[14] What might have happened in the nineteenth century if the liberal revolutionary movement of 1848 had been stronger? Germany might conceivably have avoided the path of reactionary modernization from above which contributed not only to the First World War but also to the catastrophe of Nazism. A somewhat stronger case can be made in connection with the brief revolutionary upsurge that preceded and followed the end of the First World War. Though this upsurge did run counter to powerful tendencies within the German labor movement, for a brief time it was quite widespread due to general disgust with the war. What could have happened had this wave been able to join forces with the revolutionary upsurge in Russia, as Lenin briefly hoped? If the communist revolution at this point in time had acquired a powerful industrial base, there is at least the possibility that the world might have been spared not only the horrors of Stalinist forced industrialization but also of Nazism. It is impossible to be sure: there might have been a bloody conflict with America and England with equally tragic consequences. But of the tragedies that did happen we are sure. As a concluding observation, we may note that the degree to which both Germany and Japan have become moderately livable countries since 1945 is in no small measure the consequence of *ersatz*

[14] My old friend Otto Kirchheimer used to speculate that the real turning point may have come with the failure of the Peasants' War in the sixteenth century. In German history the transitions to modern industrial society do seem to have come either too soon or too late—from the general standpoint argued in this book.

revolution in the form of defeat in the Second World War and
the subsequent allied occupation.

So far the discussion has stressed the cruelties that have been the
consequence of the great historical conflicts over the explicit
principles that were to govern human society. Some might call
these ideological conflicts. A careful Marxist, I imagine, would be
rather more likely to take the opposite tack and refer to them as
conflicts with genuine social content. In any case they are conflicts
over who should rule and by what rules.

There are also other forms of cruelty and conflict that have very
little to do with such principles. They do not arise out of any
movement to change the social order. Instead they are part of the
way most, and perhaps all, social orders work. This second type is
explicable in terms of what appear to be quite general sociological
processes characteristic of 1) the formation of cooperative human
groupings; 2) consequent struggles among these groups; 3) the
creation of formal and informal rules of conduct within and
among social groups; and 4) the tendencies of these rules to break
down. Because the historically specific and the recurring types of
conflict and cruelty often exist at the same time, it is frequently
very difficult to disentangle them empirically and assess their relative importance. On occasion, however, one does come upon close
to pure instances of the recurring variety. Whether humanity has
suffered more from conflicts over competing historical principles
or from those lacking such content is a moot point. Since conflict
over different principles of social life has in the past been mainly
a feature of Western civilization, it is quite possible that in the
daily life of ordinary people throughout the world the recurring
and, we might say, more generic sources of cruelty and misery
have also been the more significant ones.

Let us begin the analysis, then, with the general process of group
formation among human beings. According to familiar observation, the existence of an enemy provides a firm basis, perhaps even
an essential basis, for cooperation among members of the human
species. The enemy creates cooperation where none existed and
helps enormously in sustaining this cooperation. Though the con-

nection is most obvious in the case of international politics, it applies within peacefully organized communities as well: one can notice its workings down to the most trivial levels of interdepartmental rivalries in a federal bureaucracy or an academic community. Voluntary and spontaneous aspects of cooperation on a specific task without a human enemy display the same feature of team sentiments, loyalties, group cohesiveness—along with sharp rejection of any individual whose slackness endangers the common effort. A family trying to pack the car before leaving on vacation and a group of neighboring farmers working on each other's fields to get in the hay before a storm show these traits very clearly. In these situations the task that has to be performed takes on so many of the characteristics of a common enemy as the basis of group solidarity that I at least suspect that human cooperation is impossible without some sort of a hostile and resisting target for the group's collective efforts. That, however, is an issue requiring no decision here.

Whether or not human beings have an aggressive instinct or a drive for power, recurring and, I think, unavoidable social situations put them in circumstances where they have to behave as though they had such instincts. These consequences appear in their starkest form in international politics. Here the stakes are maximal and effective restraints on the resort to aggression minimal to nonexistent. It is worthwhile to pause and examine international politics more closely because, as numerous students of the subject have pointed out, they display in an especially clear manner those recurring forms of conflict that are to a high degree independent of historically specific political principles. In such an examination we can begin to perceive a possible answer to the question that has come up so repeatedly: why are human conflicts and cruelty so very widespread in time and space if they are not the necessary consequence of some powerful biological urge? The essence of the answer that makes sense to me is that the mere existence of independent or "sovereign" political units is by itself sufficient to set in motion rivalries and insecurities that will before long have these units at each other's throats. By itself the existence of these units can generate social processes that make human beings behave aggressively. They have perhaps always had a more than adequate biological capacity for such behavior, a capacity now almost infinitely multiplied as the current outcome of cultural and social evolution.

International politics constitutes a social system in its own right with its own inherent properties, some of which are subject to fairly rapid historical changes, others of which are much more constant. The foreign policies of the elites of specific states, elites that lack support or command widely varying degrees of support, constitute the distinctive elements in an international system. They are, if one were to resort to a mechanical analogy, both the sources of energy that make the wheels go around as well as the wheels and gears themselves. As in a machine, however, it is the structural relationship of the parts to each other that gives the system its distinctive properties. One cannot understand a part by itself; one can understand it only through recognizing its place in the system as a whole. Any such social or political system is a quite genuine and quite unmetaphysical reality whose character limits the behavior of all participants through the operation of sanctions that are the product of collective behavior, i.e. not of the decision of any single unit in the system, but, to repeat, of decisions imposed by the system as a whole. (A competitive market made up of a large number of buyers and sellers no one of whom can influence the price by his own decisions exercises similar constraints.)

In international systems the main recurring feature is the ebb and flow of coalitions and counter-coalitions. When for any reason one state begins to expand its power and influence, other states sooner or later come together to oppose it. They do so even if. their domestic social structures and prevailing political doctrines are in conflict with each other. Tsarist Russia, to cite a familiar example, became the ally of the Western democracies in the First World War, and communist Russia in the second one. The overriding of moral preferences by the requirements of political realism is the staple of historical writing and requires no dilated exposition here. It is in this sense, which is not confined to international politics, that a political system imposes its own goals upon the participants in the system and thereby reproduces its essential features.

Just as a free market imposed forms of behavior upon participants
that were both rational and unavoidable from their viewpoint, but
which have led to a collective irrationality from which all have
suffered, so the mechanism of international politics has by now
imposed upon individual states forms of behavior that lead to an
enormous waste of human resources and threaten the extinction of
life on this planet. The collapse of the free market led to efforts to
impose a central authority in the place of decentralized decisions.
Far from universally accepted, these efforts have helped to maintain social cohesion, though at enormous cost. Efforts to work out
a similar solution for international politics through such bodies as
the League of Nations and United Nations have so far failed.

The crucial point in comprehending how a political system imposes its own goals is to perceive the sanctions that derive from its
workings and their effect on concrete sets of individuals. Without
effective sanctions the system cannot work. The free market of the
era of competitive capitalism could not even have taken hold unless
a fair number of people had become able and willing to act in a way
generally resembling economic man and, furthermore, were able
to force others to act that way. They had to be somewhat thrifty
and with an eye for the main chance. There have been times when
for specific historical reasons these qualities or defects of the human character failed to put in an appearance on a wide scale--or,
more precisely, to show up in strategic parts of the society from
which their possessors could force similar qualities upon others
at the same social level and complementary ones of docility and
willingness to work upon the laborers beneath them. In such cases
there was little or no competitive capitalist economic development.
These areas happen to cover large parts of the globe. On the other
hand, the sanctions that sustain the kind of political behavior that
culminates in the organized cannibalism of politics among states are
apparently both more effective and pervasive. Even if affected by
modern industrial society, war is completely independent of it. So
is the competitive struggle among independent political units that
periodically breaks down in war. The elimination of capitalism,
even of any form of modern industrial organization, evidently
would by itself accomplish nothing toward ending this form of

cruelty. Can one therefore point to sanctions that transcend the workings of industrial society that explain the ubiquity of mutual destruction?

Fundamentally the answer is, I think, quite simple: fear of conquest by a foreign enemy and all that such a conquest entails. For the political leader the consequences of this ultimate sanction are obvious: the loss of all the power, prestige, and honor that have made his life what it is. For the rest of the population the situation varies more according to concrete circumstances. There are cases on record—one thinks of the slogan "better Hitler than Leon Blum"—where considerable segments of a population may look on such an outcome with indifference or even welcome a foreign ruler as serving their interests better. But such cases are very rare. Especially in the modern world foreign conquest is likely to mean severe damage to whatever stake the individual has in the existing order. By and large the industrial revolution has enormously increased the popular stake. The existing state has become the main agency, indeed the only agency, for the achievement of all purposes by all segments of the population. Furthermore, conquest at the very least means a painful upset to the established expectations and routines of daily life.

Put differently, without his own government the ordinary citizen is likely to feel that he stands no chance whatever of achieving whatever values he holds, whereas under his own regime he stands at least some slight chance. Faced with this alternative even seriously disadvantaged individuals and groups will generally support the powers that be in a crisis. That aspect, however, is only the rational calculated core of support. To it one must add not only wont and usage, the enormous influence that a modern elite exercises over the sources of ideas and the pattern of jobs and careers. The modern citizen is caught up in a web of beliefs, expectations, and sanctions that tie him to the existing regime far more tightly than was the case with most of his peasant ancestors. Only if the strands of this web are cut one by one and replaced with other ties, could the allegiance that sustains and recreates the political system evaporate, leaving the existing system an empty shell, still yielding the echoes of diplomatic niceties and military combat.

That is exactly what the Marxists once hoped for when, before 1914, they could believe that class institutions and loyalties would, at least for the proletariat, transcend the boundaries of existing states.

Conquest by a foreign enemy is only the ultimate sanction, and in the case of great powers a very remote one. The various steps and stages in between, the calculations of whose probable consequences are the daily and even hourly task of statesmen, produce results roughly commensurate with their size and their direction towards or away from this ultimate sanction. Hence one country's acquisition of some additional source of raw materials, or of greater influence with a foreign government in preference to some potential rival, becomes a good for which statesmen strive, and their loss an evil to be avoided. It is in this sense that political leaders are compelled by the sanction of failure and the force of circumstances to act *as if* they had a power drive—which some of them may actually have.

Radicals often assert that there can be no such thing as a power drive because power is a means to other and more concrete ends. When, however, the loss of power threatens the loss of the ability to achieve any ends at all, the observation loses its force and we begin to understand why political leaders are greedy for it. Add to this consideration the fact that all political acts have very uncertain consequences, and greediness for power becomes no more than a quite comprehensible if often self-defeating search for a margin of insurance. There is, as has often been observed, no security in being just as strong as a potential rival; one has to be stronger.

International politics is pure politics or naked politics, largely free of the encumbrances of law and morality. On the other hand, it is not chaotic, but subject to observable tendencies and regularities. The same tendencies are at work in domestic politics, though they are damped down by the state's near monopoly of effective force, the effects of law, the existence of codes of morality. Beneath these dampening effects there is the same endless formation of coalitions and counter-coalitions, the formal and informal truces and establishment of working rules of conduct within and among myriad social groupings, the same tendency for these rules to break down under the strains put upon them. Once again it is necessary to emphasize that there is no necessity to draw upon psychological theories about human aggressiveness in order to explain aggressive behavior. Such behavior is the product of social organization itself. In all complex societies it appears most obviously as rule-breaking (though there is also plenty of aggression within the boundaries of the rules). Rule-breaking occurs in violent and peaceful varieties. In our own society it ranges from engaging in shady and illegal business and political practices to looting, riots, and crime in the streets. In any society a large amount of this violence and rule-breaking is "normal" in the sense that it is not an attack on the existing social order and not an effort to change this order.[15] Rather it represents, especially in modern Western society, an attempt to short-cut and circumvent the rules that are the basis of social peace, if not necessarily of social justice. The temptation to use the short cut exists because rule-breaking in the form of deceit, force, and terror is generally effective in the short run. At the same time they are ineffective and inadequate as the basis of any social order.

Hobbes recognized this contradiction when he contrasted pure politics, or state of nature where life was "nasty, brutish and short," with civil society under a strong and accepted sovereign.[16] But the contradictions remain within all forms of civil society itself. In other words, moral behavior on the part of both human groups and individuals is simply suicidal and impossible under conditions that have existed very widely and show no sign of disappearing. The prerequisite for any form of behavior that is moral is that one does not always lose out by it. The prerequisite

---

[15] Hence the romantic literary admiration for the criminal, the prostitute, the factory worker, the slum dweller, the black, the peasant, as somehow free from the hypocrisy and inhibitions of civilization, is very largely sentimental illusion. It is another matter that under certain circumstances, mainly when segments of the dominant classes get to fighting among themselves, there can be enough political dynamite lying about in the lower classes for an explosion to blow up the existing order.

[16] See *Leviathan*, Chaps. XIII, XVII.

implies the existence of social order based on reciprocal and mutually acceptable obligations, enforced against those who seek advantage through evading them. In turn it seems impossible to eliminate this form of advantage, at least short of some universal human consensus and world government, which is both utopian and objectionable because it would necessarily be absolutely static. For these reasons it is evidently incorrect to maintain that all political struggles are simply or fundamentally over moral issues. Moral issues are an unavoidable aspect of politics but they are not the whole of it. Through the fact that amoral and immoral methods promise advantage in political struggles, all politics becomes tainted with immorality. Meanwhile the attempt to avoid this taint, the search for purity, can become the greatest immorality of all, in the sense of causing the greatest suffering because it leaves the political arena open to those with the fewest scruples.

The contradiction between politics and morality, never far below the surface in so-called normal times, reasserts itself with particular vehemence in times of revolutionary change. Why is it that revolutionaries sooner or later adopt, and sometimes intensify, the cruelties of the regimes against which they fight? Why is it that revolutionaries begin with camaraderie and end with fratricide? Why do revolutions start by proclaiming the brotherhood of man, the end of lies, deceit, and secrecy, and culminate in tyranny whose victims are overwhelmingly the little people for whom the revolution was proclaimed as the advent of a happier life? To raise these questions is not to deny that revolutions have been among the most significant ways in which modern men—and in many crucial situations modern women—have managed to sweep aside some of the institutional causes of human suffering. But an impartial outlook and the plain facts of revolutionary change compel the raising of these questions as well. In my estimation the essence of the answer rests in this fundamental contradiction between the effectiveness of immoral political methods and the necessity for morality in any social order.[17] Against his opponents, whether they

[17] The distinction applies, I would suggest, to all the historical definitions of morality and immorality. But that is a big claim made with appropriate diffidence.

be a competing revolutionary faction or the leaders of the existing government, a revolutionary cannot be scrupulous about the means that he uses, if he is serious about his objectives and not merely an oratorical promoter of edifying illusions. If he refrains from using unscrupulous means, the enemy may use them first and destroy the revolution itself. Lenin was the first major revolutionary leader who openly proclaimed this terrible truth and acted upon it. Far less openly and candidly Stalin acted out the consequences: that those authorized to define revolutionary strategy and revolutionary truth will shrink to one man: the dictator.[18] Bakunin foresaw this possibility in Marxism from the beginning. So did Proudhon. After the event it is difficult to tell whether they were penetrating prophets or the authors of lucky guesses. Anarchism, on the other hand, has apparently succumbed to the opposite horn of the revolutionary dilemma: ineffectiveness.

For that matter the anarchists too share the revolutionary justification of cruelty: that the revolutionaries will be the last ones in human history to have to apply it; that *this* time the victims of violence will be only the oppressors themselves. That it is possible to break the circle of contradictions in this fashion, that one can ever put an end to the conflicting imperatives of human society is, I suspect, the greatest political illusion of them all. Mankind can expect to oscillate between the cruelties of law and order and the cruelties of changing it for as long as it leaves the globe fit for human habitation.

[18] See on this score particularly M. Merleau-Ponty, *Les Aventures de la dialectique* (Paris, 1955). To be sure, in Russia quite special and distinct historical circumstances enabled the drama to be played out to its fullest tragic consequences.

III

Of Hunger, Toil, Injustice, and Oppression

At this point, however, we encounter a new issue. Have the industrial and scientific revolutions completely altered the dimensions of the problems of war, cruelty, and oppression? According to an influential critical tradition that derives from Marx, humanity has just about solved the problem of scarcity, or has at least attained sufficient technical knowledge to be able to do so in a fairly short space of time. Therefore, according to this argument, the justifications that have so far supported historical forms of oppression are now falling to pieces. There is no more reason why some should toil and others should spin; we can all become as the lilies of the field since the classical problem of extracting a surplus from an underlying population has now been solved.

For some reasons that have already been set out and others that will appear in due course this optimistic view is not one that I am able to accept. In its basic outlines the human condition displays, I would suggest, the following traits. First of all, there are too many people. An enormous proportion of these are very hungry, particularly but by no means exclusively in the economically backward areas of the world. In the advanced areas we have a technology that is used to destroy other people. In its other uses technology makes life more comfortable and agreeable while rapidly making the planet unfit for human habitation. It is a combination which suggests that *homo sapiens* may be nearing the end of his evolutionary rope and headed for extinction. Instead of self-indulgent moaning, or enjoying the pleasures of a rather prolonged *fin de siècle* (pleasures that have begun to take on a mass form in drugs and the like), there is just a bare possibility that it might be more profitable and more pleasurable to try to discover the character and causes of our present situation. More specifically, that means trying to discover whether humanity could be on the point of overcoming scarcity, and whether so doing is likely to accomplish a great deal towards the elimination of the major miseries that human beings inflict upon each other.

Can technology then eliminate scarcity and "solve" our problems? The first point to get clear is what we might mean by "solve." In order to achieve results that the optimists anticipate it would have to accomplish the following tasks. First, it would have to make possible the near elimination of routine and stultifying forms of toil, of which work on a factory assembly line is the worst. A very great deal of agricultural work remains of this type, as anyone who has taken a summer job on even an American farm can testify. Secondly, it would have to make possible a diet for everyone that was sufficient for health and energy. The same would be true of clothing, that is, there should be enough for comfort and convenience. No human culture has been satisfied with mere comfort and convenience, not even so-called primitives, a consideration that brings us towards much larger problems whose discussion had best be postponed. In the case of adequate shelter or housing, that is even more the case: whether it is possible to define an objective minimum, in anything like the sense that it is possible to define an objective minimum diet, is even more doubtful. But for the sake of getting on to more significant issues I will here make the dubious assumption that such an objective standard is possible: i.e. that there should be protection from the elements, especially in cold climates, and sufficient conveniences of a technical variety so that the inhabitants do not have to spend more than a fraction of their time in household tasks. Finally, such a conception implies the control of disease, with a great increase in preventive medicine, though by no means the eradication of disease.[1]

Though certainty is impossible because one can never be sure what technical miracles may come along, any such prospect on a world-wide scale seems almost out of the question at present rates

[1] On the futility of eradicating disease see René Dubos, *Man Adapting* (New Haven, 1965; London, 1966), 369–388.

of population increase, or even with a static population of the size
that now exists. To attain this objective there would, I suspect,
have to be a catastrophic reduction in population. That of course
could happen due to nuclear war or perhaps some other "technical
accident." But such a catastrophe would be most likely to destroy
both the technical and cultural bases that made the objective possible, even if it did not destroy all forms of life on the planet. As
everyone with minimal literacy about these issues knows, the problem of overpopulation differs sharply between the economically
advanced and the economically backward parts of the world. In
the latter it is primarily a matter of hunger. What seems like the
simplest and most objective problem of all looks to many sober authorities like the most intractable. Despite the waste and ineffi-
ciency that are obvious, despite even a certain amount of overeating
and waste in the advanced areas of the world, there just does not
appear to be much room for maneuver. Hence, even if one totally
rejects the American model as a standard to be attained, the prospects are rather dim. Not so long ago most of us who studied various aspects of what is loosely called economic growth, or more
generally modernization, a term that emphasizes the social, political,
and psychological aspects of this process, assumed that the process
would sooner or later extend to the rest of the world, in some form
or other. To me at least it now seems that the assumption is due for
a searching reexamination.

In the economically advanced countries, as is also more or less
widely known, the problem of overbreeding exists in a different
form from that in economically backward ones. Overbreeding is a
useful pejorative term that implies a relationship to other human
beings—and hence a cultural component—and to the physical environment. In the advanced countries it is not only our obviously
destructive use of technology but also its presumably constructive
aspects, from flush toilets through refrigerators, that with large
numbers impose a dangerous strain on the physical environment,
dangerous in the sense of contributing to human misery. To make
the point in as offensive a form as possible, there are grounds for
holding that the attractive young upper middle-class mother, driving a station wagon (nowadays often decorated with a peace

sticker) full of happy sunburned children, represents a major threat
to the prospect of a humane civilization, even one defined according to the purely negative criterion of reducing misery.[2]

There will be more to say about this issue from time to time as
the discussion proceeds. Here it is appropriate to mention some
quite general considerations to indicate that capitalism as such is
unlikely to be the central cause of the evils we have been discussing, though it has undoubtedly contributed to them. The role
of American imperialism in causing the misery of the backward
countries we can best defer to a later chapter. In the advanced
countries the automobile, the household washing machine, even the
television set, do not owe their ubiquity, I have come to believe, to
the formation of taste by a corporate elite that needs to jam goods
down the consumers' throats in order to maintain its profits and
hegemony. Rather they owe their popularity to the fact that they
free people, at least in the short run, from dependence on others.
With a car one does not have to wait for a bus or a train to go
where one wants. With a washing machine one can dispense with
outside laundries or with servants. A television set provides enter-
tainment and baby-sitting without leaving the house. But when
everyone has a car, traffic problems become enormous and frustrating. Similar frustrations and dependencies arise from other mechanical servants, if perhaps not in the same degree. Though the
capitalist democracies were the first societies to allow wide scope
to individual autonomy and greed and to feel the impact of these
contradictions, the contradictions as such transcend this particular

[2] On this, note Dubos, *Man Adapting*, 305, 307. The extent and intensity
of environmental damage obviously vary a great deal from one aspect of
modern technology to another. Furthermore, technology is constantly
changing, while the far-ranging effects may not become known for a long
time, and then at first most probably to only a few specialized scientists.
They in turn are not necessarily the best equipped to judge its social implications. The complexity of the issues and the range of skills needed to
discuss them intelligently prevent me from saying anything more about
them. On the other hand, there is an enormous challenge here for those
young people who have access to education and yet feel a despair (for
which I have considerable but not inexhaustible sympathy) that there is
nothing they can do with their lives.

set of economic and political arrangements. There are numerous signs of similar developments in the Soviet Union.[3] Thus the evidence indicates that gadget civilization is a consequence of the search for autonomy, the desire to make one's own independent decisions—ironically enough, a wish close to what many of modern capitalism's most severe critics claim to be seeking. This desire becomes self-defeating and indeed impossible with an increase in numbers. (In a moment we shall discuss the possibility of limiting and redirecting this drive for autonomy, which seems possible, though at frightening cost.) The essence of the situation is that an increase in numbers multiplies the frequency of situations in which it becomes necessary to have rules and regulations to govern human activities.

At least nowadays one of the easiest ways to perceive this connection is through the evolution of the disposal of human wastes, an approach to social history that, so far as I am aware, remains unexplored. Replacing human labor with plumbing and sewage plants evidently intensifies rather than reduces the need for more regulations. Where space is abundant, where one has to walk only a few steps into the woods, there is no need to make complicated arrangements about evacuation.[4] It is of course a different matter in villages, towns, and then cities. The coming of machines to do the work of human hands has, as everyone knows, enormously increased the scope of the problem. One tiny clue as to what the future holds in store is pending federal legislation to compel the users of small pleasure boats to refrain from discharging their toilets into the sea. Instead, they will have to store the contents in specially installed tanks, only some of which are confidently asserted to be not malodorous shipmates. In turn these tanks require com-

[3] For some of the consequences there see Marshall I. Goldman, *The Spoils of Progress: Environmental Pollution in the Soviet Union* (Cambridge, Mass., 1972).

[4] Many of the peoples described by anthropologists do surround evacuation with religious or quasi-religious prohibitions. Many such prohibitions express a fear that parts of the body may fall into hostile hands. Whether there is any clear connection between such rules and the density of population I do not know.

plex and novel shore installations for *their* discharge into over-
loaded sewage systems at every port of call. Perhaps, therefore,
there will be work for everyone to do after the final conquest of
nature.

At a more serious as well as more fundamental level it is necessary to raise the question whether the conquest of scarcity, even if
it were possible, would indeed remove the main source of misery
and oppression. To anticipate somewhat, I perceive reasons for
holding that it is a necessary condition, but very far from a sufficient one. Furthermore, the necessary cures, as already hinted at in
the discussion of population, may very well turn out to be just as
dangerous as the disease, horrible though the disease certainly is.
But once again it is necessary to be somewhat more precise in what
we are talking about. Scarcity of what? And do human beings
fight and oppress one another for reasons that can be reduced to
scarcity, even scarcity as it is variously defined (and organized) in
varying historical epochs?

If we begin with the question "scarcity of what?" it is reasonably clear that some human desires are indeed satiable. Despite the
huge variations in what people eat and the ways in which appetite
can be raised or reduced, there probably is some roughly ascertainable limit both of desires and more important, what is necessary for health and energy. Nor does the difficulty of acquiring
such habits seem altogether insuperable. Roughly the same goes for
clothing, at least according to the familiar saying that one cannot
wear two suits of clothes at once. Nevertheless, human beings can
be very unhappy if they do not have appropriate styles of clothing
and ornaments, a fact that will shortly lead us to more serious considerations, those of vanity and the desire for distinction. In the
area of sex, matters are more dubious. The evidence about whether
or not sexual jealousy can be damped down or altogether elimi-
nated, and whether males and females have an innate tendency to
seek a great deal of variety in this aspect of their lives is very far
from clear. Be that as it may, we may let the matter pass because
there are more serious obstacles to any notion of the possible elimination of scarcity. One of these is that scarcity has in some areas a
purely relational aspect, in the sense that A possesses something

simply because other people do *not* have it. That seems to be the point behind Frank Knight's observation about "the scarcity of such things as distinction, spectacular achievements, honor, victory, and power."[5] Now it is quite true that snobbish tendencies are culturally controllable, at least to a very considerable degree, as is clear from anthropological studies of *some* non-literate peoples where various sanctions keep such tendencies on a tight checkrein. Nevertheless there remains the issue of just what measures it would take to produce such a cultural mutation in the contemporary world, and what the costs might be. And there are still more powerful negative considerations. As the wars of religion show, and as we have discussed from a somewhat different viewpoint in the preceding chapter, human beings fight savagely and oppress each other cruelly over differing conceptions of what is good and what is evil, or what are the real values and purposes of human life. To reduce these conflicts to ones over material interests, even if material interests played a very large part in the course of the actual fighting, is in my judgment a grievous and highly misleading error. Finally, there is the highly intractable problem of order, about which it has been necessary to speak in the preceding chapter and which it will be necessary to discuss in varying contexts many times again. The historically prevailing definition of scarcity, one might say, derives as often from the "solution" to the problem of political order as it does the other way around. The Roman Republic and early Empire, it is reasonably clear, did not expand in search of slaves.[6] Rather the slave economy arose as a by-product

---

[5] Cited in Edward C. Banfield, *Unheavenly City* (Boston, 1968), 240.

[6] By classical times, and probably considerably earlier, the amount of resources devoted to war display and oppression was sufficiently large to indicate that if human beings had really wanted to solve the problem of scarcity they did not have to wait for the industrial revolution. Simply by keeping down their numbers, for which crude yet reasonably effective methods have been known since primitive times, and by managing to live in peace with each other, they might well have achieved a standard of living with enough to eat and adequate shelter against the elements. It will not do to assert that at this stage of human history human beings had not yet learned to want this kind of social order. As early as Hesiod and Aristophanes, not to mention the figure of Thersites in the Iliad, there are many

of the series of victorious wars that the Romans fought against their neighbors. If we accept the high probability of some form of armed political competition over the foreseeable future—whether this competition be between small or large units does not matter in this connection—the prospect of eliminating scarcity, or more exactly the constant redefinition of what is scarce, seems almost impossible. On balance it seems closer to the mark to regard political rivalry and competition as the cause of scarcity, rather than the other way around. As argued above, the mere fact that independent political units exist is quite sufficient to set the process of political competition in motion. Political competition is also one of the more obvious reasons for the continuous upward revision of historical conceptions of necessity and scarcity.

These considerations do not imply that something one could call a cure for excessive numbers and what we can loosely call the worship of gadgets or, even more loosely, the consumer society may not exist. Essentially it would involve a cultural mutation and a series of social conflicts, similar to that which produced capitalist industrial civilization, but this time working in the opposite direction. But it would be well to count some of the probable costs in human suffering before plunging into the process with a full head of emotional steam. Granting most of the horrors that now exist, though not all of the radical diagnosis of their causes, I can perceive rather powerful reasons for holding that the balance in terms of human suffering would scarcely be a favorable one. That there may be other possibilities too is an issue we shall come to in due course.

Because of the numbers of people that already exist on this planet and because of the ways in which they already depend upon each other for the exchange of goods and services, any substantial failure of the existing technical apparatus, including the failure to staff it adequately, could, if it happened suddenly, produce as many deaths as a major war, even a nuclear war if the failure were complete and prolonged. Furthermore, a cultural mutation that pro-

---

indications that the masses hated their oppressors and yearned for a peaceful, idealized version of the life they already led.

duced a new definition of scarcity and abundance would have to sustain itself by totalitarian and terrorist methods unless it had somehow managed to win over the overwhelming mass of the world's population in advance. In the light of the fact that even in the advanced countries there are very large numbers of people who are still making vigorous efforts to achieve some degree of participation in gadget culture, it seems highly unlikely that the necessary degree of popular support for such a change could be achieved. Even if a new conception of scarcity and abundance took hold, there would remain the very difficult problem of controlling subversive tendencies. All pre-industrial societies have had their share of traders and "operators," men who sought out crannies and openings in the prevailing social structure through which they could feather their nests and advance their position in the world by the arts of flattery, manipulation, as well as more creditable ones of sheer ingenuity and energy. Except in parts of Europe strong aristocracies managed to keep them in check. To prevent similar tendencies after a cultural and social transformation there would have to be a powerful and effective mechanism for the allocation of social tasks. Unless all tasks become pleasant ones—and we cannot have enough machines for that on account of other reasons— the whole prospect begins to smell of caste. At the very least it would scarcely be "doing your own thing." Furthermore, a rational allocation and use of the world's resources according to a new definition of scarcity implies a central world-wide authority. Computer technology, if it were allowed to continue, might some day ease the enormous technical tasks that would still remain. Nevertheless, in the light of other considerations just mentioned, including the control of recurring subversive tendencies, one can detect the possibility of a highly authoritarian world dictatorship. The result looks to me more like another Egypt than the New Jerusalem, if it succeeded, a prospect that presently seems most remote.

The future picture is not a great deal more favorable if one sets the objectives somewhat lower and perhaps a trifle more realistically. Even under the most favorable assumption of a continuing and more effective revolt against the cruelties and irrationalities of modern industrial society, a revolt that sooner or later profoundly transforms civilization as we know it without producing a cataclysm of its own, viable social units would have to be quite large. And they would have to exchange goods and services with each other. Combined with the existence of a world population that continues to rise and the unlikelihood of a reduction of the standard of living in advanced industrial countries without the use of terrorism, the prospect of what would amount to politically independent states that are economically interdependent yields a fair guarantee that human beings will continue to make each other miserable for a long time to come. At least there is no reason for alarm at the prospect that war and misery with all their beneficial effects upon morality and the social order will soon disappear.

In fact, after a revolutionary transformation of human demands sufficient to satisfy the most ascetic enemies of the affluent society, there would still have to be some equivalent of international trade. Differences in climate, great inequalities in the distribution of the earth's physical resources make it a near certainty that exchanges of goods and services over long distances will remain a prerequisite for anything recognizable as civilization. Perhaps that is another way of asserting that the problem of scarcity will always be with us, although in a form closer to the way the modern economist sees such matters than the way radical social critics do. Instead of extracting a surplus from an underlying population the basic social problem would indeed become the rational allocation of goods and services to those uses that would best satisfy human needs. As Engels put it, the day of the administration of things would have replaced exploitation.

Now on the basis of experience we do have some knowledge about what conditions are necessary to make a system of peaceful exchanges work, and more important, what forces are liable to prevent it from working. With appropriate modifications, the model of the free market economy, and what has happened to the model and the reality it was intended to explain, can tell us a great deal about what to expect. The free market was after all a device for coordinating the activities of large numbers of separate human actors without coercion and in the rational pursuit of material aims.

In order to work, the following conditions would have to be present: the participants in the system have to be approximately equal in strength. No single participant can be so strong as to dominate the others for any extended period of time. That means a) that there must be certain restraints upon the participants that the exchange system automatically imposes—such as the prospect of bankruptcy or economic failure as the eventual sanction for a series of "wrong" moves in a market economy, and b) that the participants have to a great extent internalized the rules and objectives of this particular social system in such a way as to minimize the need for coercion. Nineteenth-century bourgeois culture in its more philistine manifestations did of course precisely that for competitive capitalism. Bringing these considerations together we can see that there must be no strong temptation to disregard the rules of the game, no great prospect that the realistic thing to do is kick over the card table and sweep all the chips into one's own pocket. In a "successful" case one reason why this temptation is not very strong is that all the participants in the system share enough common values and have acquired sufficiently similar personalities and outlooks on life so that each of them has fairly effective internal checks against the temptation to engage in predatory behavior. Needless to say, such a system has never existed in anything like a perfect form; there has never been anything more than tendencies one can project in order to imagine how it might possibly work.

Though such controlled imagination is a very long way behind controlled experiment in reliability, it seems safe to say that these conditions are not likely to be met even after the revolutionary future made possible according to some radical interpretations of the present. This, be it noticed, is *not* an argument based on a conception of unchanging human nature, the usual standby of pessimistic conservatism. Rather it is an historical and sociological argument. Accepting the radicals' view of the future as composed of smaller units than the oppressive giant states with their huge bureaucracies, accepting the prospect that technological advance can eliminate some of the necessity for toil, accepting the prospect that human nature may undergo very marked changes and has already begun to show signs of reluctance to accept the discipline of a limited technological rationality, my argument asserts that the problem of order remains intractable and that failure to solve it is liable to lead to the recurrence of predatory solutions. Whatever new social units may emerge from still unimaginable transformations, they will still have to be fairly large. They will still be very unequally endowed with natural and human resources. And perhaps most important of all, as a legacy of their previous history they will have very different cultural inheritances and political personalities. For such a new system to work, the political units that composed it would have to be a collection of Swedens and Switzerlands, not a pot-pourri of Swedens, Haitis, and Hollywoods. To paraphrase one of Marx's early observations, liberation to be successful would have to be really complete; otherwise the same filthy story starts all over again. Without some central coordinating mechanism that would itself be oppressive like Hobbes's sovereign, the system could not maintain itself for long. There would be too much of a temptation for one of the units to resort to force instead of the mechanisms of peaceful exchange, to indulge in predatory behavior. Furthermore, it would require only one such unit to force the others to adopt protective measures and start the familiar historical cycle all over again.

In any event if the increase in numbers does not level off and decline sharply, human life will have to become more organized and controlled, less "authentic," spontaneous, independent, and anarchic—or else face unprecedented catastrophe. Some two generations ago a distinguished anthropologist observed dryly that *homo sapiens* was a species of anthropoids trying to live like ants, and not doing very well at it, as any philosophical observer could attest. That seems to be our fate. Since then even more powerful and obvious reasons have appeared for doubting that this peculiar quirk of the evolutionary process would enjoy a permanent success.

Ants, on the other hand, so far as we know, do not suffer from injustice and oppression, which seems to be mainly a prerogative of *homo sapiens*. But what do these words mean? As pointed out earlier, according to the positivist and relativist tradition still powerful in social science—and which has significant achievements to its credit—such words are so loaded with subjective feelings and special pleading that, along with the word exploitation they should be taboo in scientific discourse. These objections deserve serious consideration. One can scarcely read through the day's newspaper or listen to five minutes of any political speech (in any country) without finding cosmic conceptions of justice invoked in the service of the most crassly selfish objectives. Likewise, any competent historian and anthropologist can overwhelm the reader with examples of people whose standards of justice, and injustice, legitimate authority and oppression are very different from those of middle-class white Americans.

Yet these very facts looked at in a slightly different way may give us exactly what we are looking for, some universal human propensity, some constant, that allows the investigator swimming about in confusion to drop his feet to the ground and begin struggling towards terra firma. There is good evidence for a common substratum of universal human feelings that one can call the sense of injustice. All non-literate peoples about which I have read are capable of reacting with some sense of outrage when someone both injures them and violates the moral principles of their community. Civilized people, who are often more barbarous than non-literates, can carry this reaction to a point that becomes qualitatively different. Among them too, on the other hand, are obviously similar reactions. Neither ordinary communists nor ordinary Westerners like to be victims of police rage, or to hear the tramp of boots on the staircase at night that means prison or concentration camp.

On reflection it is not too difficult to discern the basis of this substratum of common human feeling; and to realize that they are not the reflection of any simple biological instinct. Human societies are after all made up of individuals who have accepted—if only in part, and by no means always willingly—a set of ordered relations with each other. (A human being who managed to grow up and survive in complete isolation from other human beings would be unlikely to develop any sense of injustice.) There are recurring and routine activities, a division of labor, a life cycle for the individual. Some of these activities are unpleasant; some may indeed be very painful, as in the case of initiation rites in non-literate so-

cieties. But an experience that is both painful and has no justification within the routine of social life is something else again and is
liable to produce an angry response. The experience of living in
society produces in human beings a distinction between legitimate
and illegitimate authority.

This observation leads directly to the vexed question whether it
is possible to give the term exploitation an objective meaning, that
is, a meaning independent of the feelings, preferences, and even
whims of the parties to any given social relationship. Though the
atmosphere has been changing in recent years, most social scientists who pride themselves on their objectivity shy away from the
word exploitation because they are inclined to regard it as a purely
emotive term. In turn this avoidance taboo has crippling effects in
making it very difficult to characterize accurately some of the most
significant social facts in nearly all human societies. With the help
of the concept of reciprocity I think it is possible to make the
term much more precise and useful, even if it seems impossible to
remove all the penumbra of emotive vagueness.

As a useful working definition we can say that exploitation forms
part of an exchange of goods and services when 1) the goods and
services exchanged are quite obviously not of equivalent value, and
2) one party to the exchange uses a substantial degree of coercion.
In assessing such matters it is necessary to take into account a
whole range or set of exchanges, not a single transaction. Collect-
ing taxes, for example, would not be exploitation where the state
and its rulers provided justice, protection, and in modern times
decent public services. It goes without saying that there are wide
grey areas between fair exchanges and exploitation. International
trade carried out under the guns of an imperialist power is obviously exploitative. But for a rich country to buy raw materials
cheaply in a poor country may not necessarily be exploitative if the
raw materials are actually cheaper in that country because they are
more abundant and require less labor to make them available.
Naturally the parties to any set of exchanges have vested interests
that make it very hard for them to agree on whether the relationship is exploitative or fair. Also they may be very unequal in their
knowledge of the relevant facts and even the capacity to make the

relevant discriminations. However, it appears necessary to proceed on the assumption that a relatively disinterested observer could, on the basis of reasonable inquiry, make adequate distinctions most of the time. To believe otherwise forces one to hold that human society has never been and never *can* be based on anything but a mixture of force and fraud. Enormous as has been the influence of these aspects of human civilization, I do not think this pessimistic view warranted by the evidence. That accepted standards change, and have good reason to change under new circumstances, goes without saying. All that I would maintain is that there is a useful middle ground between the "rightist" view that no existing relationship is exploitative and the "leftist" one that practically all existing ones display this character.[7]

If the experience of living in human society is sufficient to teach human beings some general distinction between legitimate and illegitimate authority, it is still true that systems of legitimate authority (which are *not* necessarily forms of rational authority) vary enormously over time and place: Trobriand chiefs, Hindu caste councils, doctors in a hospital, secret police interrogators, and air traffic control officers all belong to systems of legitimate authority.[8] Three elements, it appears to me, constitute such a system. When we understand what happens to each of these three and their relationship to each other, we can understand what is happening to a system of legitimate authority, including challenges and

[7] This version of the "rightist" view may be confined to social scientists. The reactionary small employer generally claims that it is the poor who gull the rich by slacking on the job, poor workmanship, and many other devices to assure that they are paid more than they are worth. I see no reason to believe that this is something that can never happen. Indeed, the lower orders probably do exploit their betters in quite a number of specific contexts. But, as indicated above, to form a realistic judgment it is necessary to take into account the total context of all these relationships.

[8] Following Weber, I use legitimate in a morally neutral sense to describe the acceptance of authority for whatever reason. Thus Hitler's authority was legitimate for those who believed in his mission. One can then of course criticize the grounds of this or any acceptance by analyzing or attacking the three elements of authority discussed in succeeding paragraphs. If the attacks convince enough people and the right ones, the authority loses its legitimacy.

attacks upon it. These three elements also, I think, make it possible to distinguish between more and less rational forms of authority.

The first element is that of reciprocity. Those who have legitimate authority either perform or claim to perform certain services, such as making the crops grow abundantly or controlling the fluctuations of the business cycle, that are believed to be essential to the welfare of the group. By obedience those subject to authority reciprocate with their services and make their contribution to the accepted conception of welfare. The same reciprocity holds among those attempting to promote a principle of counter-legitimacy, as appears in the discipline of underground revolutionary organizations. Even criminal bands that do not attack the existing principles of legitimacy in the larger society, but merely short-cut or circumvent their operation, display the same reciprocal relationship between leaders and led.

The second element is a judgment of competence that the followers make about the ways those in authority carry out their obligations. Frazer has made famous the practice of killing the king for failure to perform such duties as making the crops grow. In democratic governments the turning out of office of those leaders who have had the misfortune of facing a severe downturn in the business cycle shows many similar characteristics.

The third element is the acceptance by those who obey of the goals for which the group exists. As Sumner pointed out in *Folkways*, some conception of welfare forms part of the acceptance of group discipline, formal and informal. The acceptance can vary from the passive and diffuse attitudes of many citizens of the modern, formally democratic state to that of enthusiastic frenzy.

To trace out what has happened to these elements and why, for any extended period of human history, would not be an appropriate task for these pages. Only some general trends and their implications require attention. Though reciprocity apparently remains as a constant feature in the course of social evolution, its meaning undergoes very important historical changes. This alteration is the result of changes in the type of socially necessary services that those in authority render and, perhaps even more important, the capacity of those subject to authority to evaluate these services.

The evolutionary sequence from medicineman, shaman, and rain maker to the modern meteorologist and doctor illustrates the relationship nicely. As people realize that the shaman and priest actually do not control the weather, these figures lose their sacred awe and authority. This authority passes to the scientist, and the less a person understands about science the more he retains towards the scientist remnants of the older attitude of awe tinged with hostility and distrust, as we see in the old Russian practice of beating the priest if he failed to bring rain. In a nutshell, modern man does not know why *not* to believe. In the course of cultural evolution a new authority resting on a superior basis is necessary to cast out the old one. Only in part has this new authority arisen through the slow and painful growth of rationality.

Another change is at least equally significant. Non-literate people, so far as I have been able to learn, may resent specific acts of injustice, specific violations of their moral code. They may even, as Malinowski has demonstrated, feel very acutely the conflicts generated by two conflicting aspects of their social structure and long to disobey the requirements of duty. But they do not reject *in toto* the social system under which they live, the goals of their community and its moral standards, as has happened only in relatively modern times. Nor do they develop standards of counter-legitimacy. It is from these aspects of efforts to speed up social change, as through communism, and to prevent its taking place, as through reactionary movements including fascism, that the most acutely felt injustices and the most severe forms of coercion arise in modern times.

Behind these current struggles there are deeper and recurring political issues: the meaning of rational authority and the problem of *quis custodiet*. Authority would be both legitimate and rational where each of the three elements, reciprocity, competence, and group goals were as rational as possible in terms of the best available knowledge.[9] Given the goal of a safe passage at sea, the authority of the ship's captain over the behavior of passengers and

[9] On rationality in relation to the best available knowledge see V. Pareto, *The Mind and Society* (New York, 1935), I, 76–77 (¶ 149). (I have not seen the English edition, London, 1967.)

crew is perfectly rational, provided that the captain is technically competent and limits his orders to matters having to do with the safety and comfort of the passengers. In return for the implicit obedience on these matters, especially in times of danger, the passengers have a right to expect as safe a passage as the art of seafaring and shipbuilding will allow. The captain has a perfect right to compel a passenger to close his porthole in bad weather even if the ship's ventilation system has broken down, to order passengers curtly off the deck if seas threaten to break aboard, and need not display great social polish in seeing that these and many other orders get carried out with dispatch. On the other hand, if he abuses his authority to seduce a passenger's wife, the husband might feel a justified sense of outrage.

In such an example it is not very difficult to see the relationship among the three elements and to make judgments of rationality or lack of rationality. That is chiefly because the goal of the group in this illustration is a simple instrumental objective, and sufficient knowledge exists for attaining it.

The main difficulties in making a judgment of rationality occur when such is not the case. In political matters, at least the interesting ones, there is seldom, if ever, a single instrumental goal upon which all members of the society are in full agreement. Indeed, the essence of politics is conflict over group objectives and areas of unavoidable uncertainty about how to attain them. Is it nevertheless possible to characterize some human goals or values as rational and others as irrational? Many respected thinkers would answer this question in the negative, mainly on the grounds that a positive answer smacks of totalitarianism, forcing people to be "happy." Sympathizing with this objection I have taken the position that unhappiness and misery in certain of their major forms are objective facts, while happiness is much more fluid and subjective. This position leads to the conclusion that political goals which demonstrably lead to greater unhappiness and misery are indeed irrational, those that demonstrably lead to reducing human misery in the forms under discussion are rational.

The relation between competence and the distinctions between rational and irrational forms of political authority is somewhat easier to grasp. Judgments of competence and incompetence change continually in accord with the development of knowledge. Among some modern liberals one encounters the view that there can be no such distinction because political events are inherently uncertain and unpredictable. For them the mere idea of making such a distinction suggests at the very least pretentiousness and at worst totalitarian claims to omniscience. Other liberals make what is to me the naively optimistic claim that the social sciences will some day acquire the precisions of the natural sciences. Without going into the debate further I would merely urge that these general arguments obscure the possibilities that do exist for making sufficiently firm judgments for intelligent action and the possibility of improving our comprehension. What is difficult to forecast is what the state of social and political knowledge will be, let us say, two generations hence. There could be revolutionary changes in our intellectual tools that would have a powerful impact on the capacity to distinguish competent from incompetent leaders. Two generations before Marx and Freud, Durkheim and Weber, who could have anticipated their insights into human society and the new questions those who followed them would ask? By asking their questions *and* others, those who study human society today can acquire knowledge about basic social trends. Such knowledge does not assert what the future has to be. But it can tell us that certain lines of policy are unpromising and liable to increase the sum total of human misery—or that of specific social groups. For instance, Western policies towards Asia that take no account of agrarian relationships, and that interpret Asian societies solely in terms taken from a dubious view of Western liberal experience are, I submit, symptoms of political incompetence or deliberate deception, or both.

This observation is not a denial of the very large measure of uncertainty in serious political judgments, or even the prospect that much of this uncertainty is unavoidable because politics reflect continually emerging and in some degree inherently novel and unique historical configurations. What does deserve condemnation is the vulgarized form of Pontius Pilate's attitude in which political opponents call each other names and the observer merely decides both are about equally to blame and equally innocent, and then steps outside of the situation. The refusal to pass judgment when knowledge is available, the failure to try to find out why judgment is difficult, and to make an effort to correct the situation, constitutes intellectual and moral sloth. It is equally insufficient to assert that social and political obstacles will always prevent the effective use of social knowledge because such knowledge runs counter to vested interests. Though that may often be true, one cannot really tell when the knowledge itself is weak and poorly established.

We may now take up the ways in which the element of reciprocity aids in distinguishing between rational and irrational authority. There are many instances of pseudo-reciprocity that we can call irrational when those in authority either do not provide services in return for obedience or provide services that are neither necessary nor desirable from the standpoint of reducing human miseries. The decline of religious and magically based authority is a familiar example. There is no need to linger over this aspect except to suggest that critical understanding, if it can continue to develop, may come to very similar conclusions some day about many services (prestige, preservation of civilized values) now provided by the modern state. But that will not happen, if it happens at all, before men and women find ways of organizing social life that dispense with the sovereign state.

Violations of the principle of reciprocity are the common forms of what many people recognize almost instinctively and automatically as examples of the irrational and arbitrary application of authority. These, I suggest, fall into two main types. In one, those in authority apply compulsion or coercion that is for some reason deemed excessive, even though it is applied in support of group objectives or generally accepted social norms. The application of the death penalty for petty theft would impress many people as arbitrary and irrational today, though the recent demands to allow the police to shoot looters on sight during a riot show how the more humane attitude depends on a general degree of social stability. Thus judgments of rationality in this area involve judgments about the quality of the social order that the rules defend, as well as judgments about the effectiveness of certain kinds of punishment, all matters that are not easy to decide. In the other type, perhaps the most common of all forms of arbitrary and irrational authority, those in authority use coercion (or other methods) not in support of accepted social norms or social objectives, but in pursuit of strictly selfish objectives. The case of the ship's captain who abuses his authority to seduce the wife of a passenger would be an obvious example. Here the difficulties occur in deciding what rights, perquisites, and privileges are in actual fact necessary to encourage those in authority to execute their duties effectively. How necessary is it that socialist officials have private limousines and good apartments? That surgeons in capitalist countries charge the prevailing fees? On such matters there is far more passionate conviction than firm knowledge. Indeed, that is quite evidently the case with all aspects of the distinction between rational and irrational authority.

Hence it is hardly a wonder that the issue of *quis custodiet*, or how to control authority, has been about the most intractable of any in both political theory and political practice. There can be no effective control of authority without agreement upon the standards by which to judge the behavior of those who exercise it. We have discussed this aspect sufficiently to move on to more sociological and institutional ones. What conditions would have to prevail, what mechanisms would have to exist, in order to prevent arbitrary abuses of authority, to encourage and compel the rulers to adhere to rational principles in the exercise of authority?

According to a tradition that is at least as old as Plato's discussion of the guardians, one way to accomplish this result is to select and educate the leaders in accord with the correct principle. Except for a few non-literate societies that lack the institution of chiefs, every human society does of course select and train its leaders according to *some* principles. That is not the problem. Rather the problem is one of changing existing procedures to make them more rational. The most familiar answer is through an educational dictatorship. The actual historical experience of reigns of virtue and terror provide powerful grounds for rejecting this solution. Here, I suspect, the argument may have become stuck in a rut because of a tendency to focus too narrowly on violence.

The alternatives are not necessarily between violence and nonviolence, between a gradualism that allows prevailing horrors to grow and multiply and an educational dictatorship that would create even greater cruelty and in the end fail to achieve its purposes. Instead, the probabilities contained in existing social trends and the degrees of free choice they present are a more subtle and complex mingling of violence and other agents of social change. In the past how has change come about in the selection of a society's leaders and the principles according to which they rule? Surely in large part through violence, which has played a role in destroying institutions and even habits of mind derived from institutions that were obstacles to rationality. But that is not all. There have also been changes through the seepage of new ideas among a population, the slow ferment of critical thought. And probably most important of all there have been changes that come from alterations in the circumstances and setting of daily life that affect the whole texture of the social order. Though a great many of these changes have risen out of alterations in the modes of production and exchange, that is not their only source. More and more in modern times the acts of governments have impinged upon and altered not only the way men and women produce and exchange goods and services but other aspects of social life including the ways in which they reproduce themselves. The more changes take place through the ferment of ideas and through alterations in the circumstances of daily life, the less is the necessity to resort to violence, which by itself is ineffective.

These comments, I would agree, have about them, a somewhat disagreeable air of manipulation. On the other hand, all human society amounts to manipulation of human beings by each other. Everything depends upon who is doing the manipulating and for what purposes. Those who resist the status quo also manipulate both each other and the dominant groups. In a rational society, to repeat once more, the manipulation takes place to reduce human misery. A world of isolated human beings having no connection with each other would not only be the utmost in misery and degradation; it would actually be impossible.

Other aspects of the problem of controlling authority, preventing or diminishing arbitrary abuse and irrational coercion have to do with arrangements that allot various kinds and degrees of power and authority to other elements in the population. All of them are liable to develop irrationalities of their own. It is also wise to recall that sheer disorder, the absence of any effective political authority, has been itself a major cause of misery for long portions of human history. Because ordinary men and women have left very few records, we cannot be sure that they generally preferred the exactions of a harsh monarch who repressed disorder and brigandage to the depredations of a host of petty tyrants. Furthermore, ordinary people had rather little real choice in the matter. In more recent times this issue has died out for most of the world. Whatever else one could say against modern governments as they developed in both east and west, there appears to be no reason to doubt that public order existed most of the time. Now, however, the situation shows signs of changing. Since we are still discussing the problem of *quis custodiet*, this is not the point at which to speculate on those forms of modern society without *custodies* or with inadequate ones. Nevertheless, it is a consideration to keep in mind in analyzing checks on authority, or more precisely, systems of authority that claim to incorporate self-correcting features against the irrational abuse of authority.

Again, according to a very old tradition, in this case supported by a substantial body of experience, a distribution of property that avoids sharp extremes of wealth and poverty helps to create a general political climate opposed to the arbitrary abuse of authority. Though equality of possessions is by no means necessary, the distribution would have to be one that ruled out Anatole France's famous jibe: the law in all its majesty forbids rich and poor alike to sleep under the bridges over the Seine. All members of the political community, in other words, must have enough resources to enable them to participate as full-fledged citizens.

Though the discussion has usually considered property in terms of physical possessions, this aspect is not as far as I can see, essential. Rather the key point is that the ordinary citizen should possess some set of attributes that forms the basis for an effective veto over some decisions made by those with authority over him, in other words, a basis for self-respect. In addition, the ordinary citizen has to have the capacity to evaluate these decisions intelligently, i.e. to perceive more than the immediate personal consequences, a capacity that in turn implies opportunities for education as well as some leisure and reflection. Property can provide the social basis for these qualities. So also can skills under certain conditions, and skill rather than property is relevant to the modern situation. The skill has to be in demand and the situation such that those who control the demand do not completely determine the use to which the skill is put. Otherwise one can have a nation of robots. Correspondingly the possessor of the skill cannot completely control the terms of its use. If the possessor does, the situation is liable to degenerate into a series of holdups. Whether it is at all possible to attain this delicate equilibrium in a modern highly integrated economy is certainly open to serious question. If the arguments presented earlier are correct, the trend will be towards more centralized controls and less individual autonomy. Nevertheless, as indicated earlier, these trends are not inevitable: enough knowledge is available to reverse them if people really wanted to and felt confident about the results.

A second and much more conservative interpretation, found in the writings of de Tocqueville and Mosca, stresses the oligarchical nature of all known human societies of any degree of civilization, and the conflicts of interest among these oligarchies as the mainspring of any check on arbitrary power. The virtues of this viewpoint rest in its realism about the tendencies towards the abuse of power and authority, and in its effort to harness the inevitable conflicts of interest in any complex society for the sake of justice and the public interest in a more rational social order. That seems to me a valid insight despite the fact that modern proponents of this view deny the possibility of there being such a thing as a public interest. Even the defense of hereditary privilege in this standpoint may be perfectly compatible with a rational social order, since it may easily take more than one generation to cultivate a certain cast of mind and set of intellectual skills, especially among the professional classes and also among those who exercise political authority. Once gained, these skills could bring far greater benefits to the society than would absolute equality of opportunity. The fact of the matter is that here again there is very little conclusive evidence one way or another—and a great deal of strong feeling. The most it is possible to assert with some confidence is that a completely closed elite that rejected the brilliant and ambitious from the lower classes would waste large reservoirs of talent and sooner or later cause the accumulation of dangerous resentments, especially under modern conditions. But a completely fair society in which no individual could blame circumstances beyond his control for his failures and disappointments might just as easily lead to the accumulation of resentments that would tear the social fabric apart. Perhaps for this reason alone a completely rational social order is an impossibility. Since we have never had one, we cannot know, and such a distant prospect furnishes no ground for abandoning efforts to reduce and eliminate the injustices and cruelties that do exist.

Since the defects of elitist liberal pluralism have been the subject of recent able discussions by others to which I have nothing to add,[10] I shall do no more than comment briefly upon them. Essentially they amount to the fact that instead of being a safeguard against the abuse of authority the competition among elites can and has become a major source of abuses and injustices itself. That is because the competition is, according to the critics, really pseudo-competition since the elites are all in the same boat. Many more interests unite them than divide them. Indeed, their fundamental shared interest, which transcends national boundaries and to some extent even ideological ones, is to preserve the existing social order of advanced industrial societies against demands for a rational social order that in the present historical context have to be revolu-

[10] See Wolff, "Beyond Tolerance," in Robert Paul Wolff, Barrington Moore, Jr., and Herbert Marcuse, *A Critique of Pure Tolerance* (Boston, 1965; London, 1969); Michael Paul Rogin, *The Intellectuals and McCarthy: the Radical Specter* (Cambridge, Mass., and London, 1967), and Herbert Marcuse, *One-Dimensional Man* (Boston and London, 1964).

tionary. On this last point the argument hinges on the conception of rationality. If one defines rationality in such a way as to imply a social order that differs absolutely from anything that has ever existed, the revolutionary conclusions follow automatically, though not necessarily the revolution itself, or at least not one that brings about the hoped-for results.

Elitist pluralism is a conservative answer to the issue of *quis custodiet*. Direct democracy and, more recently, the neo-anarchist notion of participatory democracy are radical answers. Direct democracy brings to mind the theory and practice behind such experiments in popular control as the meetings of the Paris sections of the *sans-culottes* during the brief period well prior to Robespierre's fall when they had some real power, and also the Russian soviets during a period that was also very brief when they exercised some real power. According to William Hinton's account, basically similar practices existed in the Chinese village he was able to observe during the early stages of that revolution.[11] He describes very vividly how the local communists called together the inhabitants of the village to discuss certain aspects of the redistribution of land that were to have profound effects on their lives, and how the group broke up into separate units of buzzing discussion about each point, to come together afterward for a decision.

A key point in all these arrangements is that they did provide an opportunity, even if by no means a full one, for the victims of the social order to make their own voices heard. At this point in time revolutionary terror had temporarily removed from the arena that portion of the political spectrum that in "normal" times is the most articulate, namely of course the old elites. But in a very short space of time revolutionary terror turned against direct democracy. The usual explanation is the necessity for the restoration of order, the impossibility of taking into account by such means the general requirements of the whole society, of reaching and coordinating decisions through myriad separate groups of un-

[11] See his *Fanshen: A Documentary of Revolution in a Chinese Village* (New York, 1966; London, 1967).

educated people. That is indeed a crucial part of the story. But it leaves out of account whose law and order was restored and to whose benefit the restoration took place. In general, it is safe to assert that the restoration of order and security has not been for the benefit of the little people in whose honor the revolutions were proclaimed. Nor is it possible, I think, to separate the original use of the revolutionary terror against the old elite from its later use against the little people. Direct democracy generates revolutionary terror, its own nemesis.

Participatory democracy represents an attempt to preserve the virtues of direct democracy while divorcing it from revolutionary dictatorship and terror. As far as I am aware, the term became common through use by the American radical student movement, many of whose members were acutely conscious of the authoritarian trends in Russian communism. By 1969 many student radicals had become disillusioned with participatory democracy, as experience had revealed the necessity for discipline and deception, the iron law of revolutionary politics as well as of any other politics. If that were all there were to participatory democracy, it would hardly be worth discussing here. That, however, is not the case. In addition to its inherent interest as an effort to escape from the authoritarian nemesis of previous revolutionary movements, participatory democracy shows many affinities with other movements, such as that for self-management in parts of Eastern Europe, Algeria, and also under Western capitalism.

The common assumption that these movements share constitutes one of the possible answers to the question *quis custodiet:* the individual can exercise control over authority by participating in decisions, particularly decisions affecting his own life. Furthermore, no one has a right to make decisions that affect the individual without allowing this individual to take part in making this decision. This principle is morally very attractive to anyone brought up under the influence of Western conceptions of individual freedom and autonomy. Let us therefore analyze its implications and feasibility. As with the other answers to the problem of *quis custodiet* we should try to learn what we can from efforts to put the principle into practice, at the same time keeping carefully in mind the historically limited and therefore tainted character of such evidence.[12]

For sharing in the ordering and arrangement of the work process to have any real meaning, those who do the work must have certain skills and qualifications that those in higher authority respect. There must also be more than one possible way of performing a task if the workers' own decisions are to have realistic meaning. Where these conditions exist there is likely to be considerable *de facto* participatory democracy. Such conditions do exist rather widely, not only in extensively surviving crafts, such as carpentry and plumbing, but also in those areas where new technologies are entering rapidly, chemical industries and electronics.[13] All these conditions have nothing to do specifically with socialism, or capitalism. *De facto* participatory democracy can exist to a high degree under both. It has little or nothing to do with the fundamental political character of a regime. Though it does contribute to human dignity and is not something to be despised, sharing in decisions is no panacea, no general cure for the evils of injustice and arbitrary power.

In the form of self-management (*autogestion*) the notion is, I shall try to show, inherently contradictory and impossible to realize in practice. Partial imitations, on the other hand, have an element of built-in intellectual dishonesty because they claim too much. The main difficulty with self-management on any wide scale is that the procedure as such contains no way to take account

[12] Tainted in the sense a) that in the absence of experimental methods allowing replication and control of individual variables it is impossible to isolate the clear-cut causal or functional relationships among two or more variables and b) that in the course of further historical development the obstacles which make the application of some principle seem to us permanently utopian may disappear—or be replaced by new obstacles. There is truth in the observation that we do not know how Christianity really works because it has never been tried. The same applies to democracy, socialism, and anarchism. There is a difference between inherent unfeasibility and powerful enemies that is easy enough to perceive in logic but very difficult to disentangle in actual sociological and historical investigation.

[13] See Robert Blauner, *Alienation and Freedom: The Factory Worker and His Industry* (Chicago and London, 1964).

of the larger requirements of the whole society. It cannot solve the general problems of social order. Each individual plant or economic unit tends to pursue its local and selfish interests, as has been repeatedly discovered in practice. Pushed to its logical conclusion, when these selfish interests balance each other without outside intervention the system would amount to no more than the classic model of competitive capitalism ruled by an impersonal market. As a practical matter under socialism, it may be a very good device to leave a considerable degree of autonomy to individual plants to carry on production within the framework of some overall plan and one in which these plants have some voice in drawing up, as they did in practice even in the most totalitarian phase of the Soviet experience. But then there is no use pretending that real self-management or workers' control exists, because fundamental decisions are made elsewhere. Likewise, there may be highly desirable features in André Gorz's proposal that the workers in regions allowed to stagnate because of profit considerations under capitalism get together and insist on a more humane use of the area's natural and human resources.[14] In their essentials, however, such actions are no different from the tugging and hauling among competing interest groups that take place under pluralist democracy. In effect, then, self-management is a device to oppose the abuses of the powers that be, capitalist or socialist. It is not a possible substitute for a central authority.

Furthermore, sharing in the decision-making process does not automatically diminish suffering or raise the level of human dignity. Beyond a certain point it can have quite the opposite results. *Homo committicus*, to coin an appropriate barbarism, is not the only species of *homo sapiens* and not necessarily the most admi-

[14] See his *Stratégie ouvrière et néo-capitalisme* (Paris, 1964; English translation, *Strategy for Labor*, Boston, 1967). Gorz also foresees a situation in which these local struggles for power turn into more serious battles that an American might call confrontations. By winning a series of these the workers might eventually, he asserts, attain to real power in the state. Though I see little prospect for this outcome in the USA, the general issues of political strategy that he raises transcend the question of participatory democracy and will receive consideration below.

rable one.[15] A very precious part of human freedom is that *not* to make decisions. What would life be like if it were necessary to attend a meeting every day to decide at which hour the street lights should go on? What would happen if every time two cars met on the road their drivers had to discuss on which side they would pass each other? Is there any sensible reason why the passengers on an airplane should want to participate with the pilot and airport officials in decisions about landing and take off? To choose a somewhat more interesting and ambiguous case, just what should be the patient's share in a decision to undergo a difficult and dangerous operation? All these cases bring out the fact that there are huge areas of life where the point is *not* to share in a decision. In some, such as which side of the road one drives on, the nature of the decision is completely indifferent. All that matters is that there should be *some* decision. In others the problem is simply to get the right decision according to some easily agreed upon criterion. In such areas it is possible to formulate standards of competence about ways to make the decision, and, with considerably greater difficulty, find ways to enforce them. In still other areas of life it may be impossible to persuade people to accept clear criteria that distinguish between good and bad decisions. All through this essay, for example, we have been trying to apply the criterion of minimal suffering to assess political arrangements and have also argued that this is in fact the criterion people generally try to apply. But there is no cosmic reason why they have to apply it. Where for any reason people fail to agree on a criterion, the only solutions are to fight the matter out, in the end by killing each other if the issue seems that important, such as the nature of the trinity or the virtues of liberal democracy and communism.

This review of those aspects of social structure and more narrowly political arrangements that Western experience has presented as possible answers to the problem of *quis custodiet* shows that none of them work very well. All of them can become the

---

[15] See Michael Walzer, "A Day in the Life of a Socialist Citizen," in his *Obligations: Essays on Disobedience, War, and Citizenship* (Cambridge, Mass., 1970), 229–238.

source of their own forms of abuse of power. What "answers" there are to this formidable query have arisen from within the liberal democratic tradition. The basic reason is a simple one: there can be no other power with which to check those in authority than that derived from the people or specified segments of the people.

Revolutionaries have no independent answers. What answers they offer they have acquired from earlier phases of liberal democracy. As the expression "social democracy" reflects, the two movements were closely interwoven with each other during much of the nineteenth century, especially on the European continent. Revolutionary movements have no way of coping with the problem of legitimate succession to positions of authority nor with the problem of giving legitimacy to changes in policy. These problems they "solve" by fission and by violence against their own members. More precisely, what methods they do have they have borrowed as ideals from liberal democracy, but in practice they have suppressed them. Democracy within the revolutionary movement, confined to those that accept the general aims of the revolution has been the main attempt. It is evidently impossible to sustain internal democracy in practice when the revolution faces a powerful enemy in the form of widespread popular opposition, either before taking power or afterward. Lenin faced this issue more clearly than most. But even he equivocated by turning against democracy when his authority was challenged, and demanding its strict application on the rare occasions when he found himself temporarily in the minority. The legend about his being less authoritarian than Stalin stems from the fact that he was lucky enough to die before Russia had to face the crises of socialist construction.

The defender of socialism can object that repressive socialism of the Russian variety is the consequence of specific and historically limited conditions. It arose in a backward country and in opposition to an autocratic regime, factors that imparted to it from the very beginning an autocratic taint. Secondly, it came to power without the support of the mass of the population, in this case the peasants. Finally, it was compelled to carry through industrialization at break-neck speed in a hostile international environment. Presumably under more favorable conditions socialism might be more humane. One cannot rule out this possibility. But if it does come to pass, socialism will have to conquer obstacles inherent in its own tradition, or rather face problems for which its tradition provides no adequate answers.

Marxian or centralized socialism has no answer to the query *quis custodiet*. The notion of transferring control over the means of production to the people or to society as a whole is an empty slogan. It says nothing about what people are to take charge of production. It gives no more than the faintest guidance about what policies they should follow. And it tells us nothing about how the leaders and policies can be changed by those human beings who are their victims. This failure to answer the query *quis custodiet*, I think, is the fatal flaw at the heart of the whole socialist remedy for human ills.

There are other flaws too that are scarcely less baneful and the source of a continuing repressive tendency in socialist practice. Any allocation of material and human resources that goes against the wishes of a substantial segment of the population—and here we are *not* talking about the rich—requires a repressive apparatus. That is true even when some combination of historical and philosophical algebra enables those who make the decisions to claim that ultimately they are for the benefit of the society as a whole, an algebra that of course every dominant class creates for itself. But, to repeat, under socialism there is no legitimate opportunity for the lower orders to check the calculations or even express overt suspicion about them. Communists are far less compassionate about the victims of historical "progress" (witness the liquidation of the kulaks and the purge trials) than were even the most self-righteous and self-confident nineteenth-century capitalists.[16]

There is one more closely related consideration that deserves our attention. The figure of the trader, or more broadly the person who seeks opportunities for personal gain by living in the interstices

[16] Marx's letters on India give full expression to this cruel complacency. Confidence in one's historical mission as the *avant-garde* of a new civilization or the defender of an existing one evidently does a great deal to obliterate the sight of human suffering, no matter what specific form this confidence may happen to take.

of the social order and manipulating them for his own advantage through satisfying others who cannot get what they want, is a universal one in civilized societies. He existed all over pre-modern Asia as well as Europe and throughout antiquity. Capitalism is of course unique in trying to organize human society around him through the market, and the judgment that it doesn't work any more is certainly a respectable one. Nevertheless any conceivable society is likely to have to face the problem of either finding a niche for such persons, a role for them that diminishes the total suffering in the society, or else going to great lengths to suppress them. That too is a problem for which the socialist tradition provides no adequate answer. Nor for that matter does any leftist tradition at present, because all of them are steeped in anti-capitalism.

As early as the days of Proudhon and Bakunin the anarchists foresaw the oppressive possibilities inherent in Marxian socialism and warned against them long before they became live issues on the historical agenda. On the other hand, the anarchist tradition too, in my judgment, lacks any feasible answer to the problem of social order. Fundamentally the anarchists seek to solve the problem of *quis custodiet* by eliminating any central authority, which under twentieth-century conditions I hold to be impossible. Only a few years ago hardly any serious writer about politics would have bothered to challenge such a conclusion. One could dismiss the heirs to the anarchist tradition as no more than stubborn misguided and scattered adherents of an obsolete doctrine. That is no longer the case, even if its contemporary adherents are for the most part unaware of their intellectual ancestors. While the current neo-anarchist revival may turn out to be an ephemeral phase, a turn of affairs I rather doubt because it does appeal to a mood and set of needs created by modern industrial society, and which we are now able to recognize in many other manifestations, including even the pseudo-radical aspects of fascism, the matter deserves discussion. Proposed remedies reveal a great deal about social pathology even when they cannot cure it.

Though anarchism is a rather loose term that covers a variety of sins or virtues, depending on one's viewpoint, it is possible to discern a common objective. This objective is to reorganize human society into a series of autonomous communities. (Communitarianism might be a better term than anarchism, especially for its contemporary manifestations, though I prefer neo-anarchism in order to avoid an ugly neologism. For present purposes there is no need to distinguish between those who advocate violence and those who repudiate it, as this larger issue will be discussed at length later.) Though there are wide variations in program and practice, there is a common stress on certain characteristics that such communities are expected to display. One is a cooperative division of labor with a heavy emphasis on warm personal relationships. Another is upon equalitarian sharing both of material goods and in the making of decisions that affect the community, though actual practice evidently varies considerably. Still a third trait is an anti-materialistic ethic that verges upon asceticism in some cases. The whole is both a mirror image and rejection of the present-day competitive and individualist capitalist ethic, or more accurately what neo-anarchists perceive this ethic to be.

As far as the purely internal arrangements of these communities go, they could probably be made to work. The popular notion that human beings have too much innate aggression for such arrangements to be feasible is almost certainly false. Anthropologists have come upon enough cases of reasonably peaceable cooperative societies to rule out this line of criticism. On other grounds it is indeed possible to criticize the anarchist ethos and program: endless discussion of small issues does not necessarily contribute to the creative development of the human personality, whatever that may mean. Actually this kind of discussion often amounts to a form of self-stultification and self-delusion. Young people who indulge in this would often be better off engaged in disciplined study, which is something they have to do for the most part by themselves. Furthermore, participation in decisions that affect one's life is not a specifically anarchist notion anyway. It is very much a part of the liberal and democratic ideal. But these aspects are not at issue here. Anarchist communities as such are within the range of general social possibilities, given the appropriate conditions. The significant difficulties have to do with the relationships of these communities to each other. That is one reason why the societies resembling the anarchist ideal which anthropologists have come upon generally enjoy some form of isolation and protection from other human societies.

The anarchist tradition has very little to offer in answer to the question of how anarchist communities could be expected to get along with each other. As I understand it, the essence of the answer holds that the experience of living in anarchist communities would produce a sufficient transformation of the human personality, reducing its competitive, aggressive, and acquisitive traits, to make possible the loosest form of federation among anarchist communities. Within this federation or set of federations there would be some division of labor and exchange of goods and services. This is an inadequate answer because it does not put the question in a sufficiently probing form.

Though the issues are interrelated, since the solution chosen for one affects the ways in which it is possible to cope with others, for the sake of convenience and clarity it is possible to analyze the general problem into at least four questions: 1) How can the type of rivalries that have so far always plagued independent political units be avoided under the situation of a series of anarchist communities? This is the classical issue of the working of balance-of-power mechanisms. It is necessary to emphasize once again that these rivalries derive from the mere existence of independent political units. They do not come about due to any human propensity to seek power: the situation itself imposes a power drive. Nor are they a consequence of scarcity. The mechanism imposes a definition of scarcity upon its participants. Furthermore, it operates quite independently of cultural stages of historical development. It has existed among American Indian tribes, the city states of classical antiquity, in China and India during periods when the central government was weak (which for India was a very large part of the time), and of course in modern times. So far the only way human beings have been able to damp down the workings of this mechanism has been through the establishment of a strong centralized state, an arrangement which has of course merely transferred the struggle to the international arena, and with modern technology made it more murderous. The control of rivalries generated by the existence of independent political units, the actual form of Hobbes's state of nature, seems to me the most formidable difficulty that neo-anarchism would have to overcome if it ever rose to the level of a realistic alternative to the status quo.

The other difficulties are also very large. Because they concern the allocation of resources we can discuss them together. 2) What may happen due to the fact that some anarchist communities will be much wealthier than others and have control of resources that others require? 3) Presumably such difficulties would be less severe in a less materialistic and partly de-industrialized world. But just how much de-industrialization and of what kind would a neo-anarchist advocate in the light of the world's population and economic interdependence? 4) Would neo-anarchist societies be able to control innate tendencies towards the growth of the trader, the manipulator and the fixer, without creating such a restrictive moral code and enforcing it by such nosy and inquisitorial methods as to cast a repressive miasma over the whole culture?

The degree of feasible de-industrialization might turn out to be the hardest question of all to answer in a way that would command assent even among neo-anarchists themselves. It is obvious that no modern city can grow enough food to feed its inhabitants and that exchanges with the countryside are necessary unless one is willing to exterminate the inhabitants of the city. These exchanges can be governed either by market relationships or by centralized allocation of goods and services (or some combination of the two), both of which the neo-anarchists reject as basic principles of social organization. The same basic consideration applies in connection with the differential endowment of neo-anarchist communities with natural resources. Suppose that one community is able to produce some good, say lettuce or oranges, that other communities badly want or need. Can one realistically expect that a new ethic will take such strong hold that the fortunate community will not try to exploit its advantage? And by what criteria *could* one decide that it was not trying to extract the most possible from this advantage? Once again we are left with the choice of either letting market forces have full play, which amounts to refraining from applying any ethical standard to the relationship, or else using some kind of *force majeure* at the disposal of a central authority to impose a pattern of distribution that was accepted as desirable on ethical and political grounds by the rest of the society. But both these choices imply a form of society very different from the anarchist ideal. For the latter to work there is evidently necessary some sort of invisible hand that is not Adam Smith's market, and certainly not the very visible hand of the bureaucratic state.

It appears that this invisible hand would have to take the form of a moral code shared by all of the new communities. It would also have to be specific enough in its anti-materialistic tenets to make possible an enormous number of decisions of the type just mentioned. Here "possible" means that ordinary human beings would be socialized in such a manner that they could quickly and easily draw the right deductions in concrete circumstances. This socialization would also have to be effective enough to prevent the emergence on any significant scale of the trader and manipulator, whose growth would quickly undermine the whole system.

Obviously nothing of the sort is remotely in sight at present. Nevertheless one cannot rule it out as a remote possibility and as perhaps the only way of maintaining peace and order in a very crowded world. Human beings are adaptive, one can almost say too adaptive, and can learn to live under very varied and strange circumstances. These circumstances, if they ever should come to pass, would on the other hand bear little resemblance to the free utopias imagined in some currents of anarchist and neo-anarchist thought. Humanity as a whole would then resemble a mass of passengers cooped up below decks on a ship in a dangerous storm: if one passenger in desperation for air reached up to open a porthole or did something else that would endanger the whole ship, other passengers would quickly and almost instinctively restrain him bodily. But there would be no safe port to which the ship was heading, and no captain upon whom one could rely for safe passage.

So far each line of thought seems to lead to a dead end. Allowing the world to continue the way it is promises intolerable human suffering. So do all proposals to change it when one follows through with their implications. We seem to be left with the

Aristotelian insight that all possible political arrangements are evil when carried to their inherent conclusions, and that the only hope is to find an appropriate mixture whereby at least some of the evil consequences will cancel each other out or minimize one another.[17] I will confess to a very considerable suspicion at reaching such a conclusion: it is rather too comforting for those who benefit from whatever happens to be the prevailing distribution of human misery. Rather than pursue this line of thought at an abstract level it will be better to drop the matter now and come back to it later in a concrete historical context, that of the contemporary United States. Furthermore, if any thinkers are going to find their way around this form of conclusion or discover a better one, human society will have to maintain conditions for free intellectual inquiry. Since these have been only too rare in human history, we will do well to discuss this general problem first.

[17] Under contemporary conditions the strongest and most optimistic argument known to me on behalf of a mixture makes these points: The conceptions of capitalism, socialism, and neo-anarchism are too global. The right of property is not a unit but a bundle of quite specific rights that varies greatly from case to case. Thus private property rights in an automobile do not extend to driving it on the wrong side of the street, through traffic lights, etc. The same is true of incentives to elicit certain forms of socially desirable behavior and sanctions to inhibit undesirable forms. Socialist societies experiment with material incentives and capitalist societies with non-material ones. From this standpoint the problem becomes one of discovering through trial and error the proper mixture of rights and incentives on a case-to-case basis, the mixture that will minimize human suffering.

Though I am willing to travel a considerable distance in company with this argument, one major difficulty impresses me. The proper mixture for one set of decisions—say the exchanges between town and countryside—has to be compatible with other sets of decisions—say the kind of industry encouraged, the form of educational system, and many others—if human suffering is really to be minimized. Hence a distinctive overall institutional pattern is bound to emerge. And that brings us right back to some variations on the major themes of capitalism, socialism, and neo-anarchism. The range of possible mixing apparently has built-in structural limits.

Of Heresy, Intellectual Freedom, and Scholarship

We have arrived at the last of the general sources of human miseries to be discussed in this essay, persecution for the expression of unacceptable ideas and beliefs. Before proceeding to a discussion of intellectual freedom in the existing world, and attacks and limitations upon this freedom, in relation to the effort to create a less irrational society, it seems especially necessary to make clear one's conception of the objective. I take the position that intellectual freedom is both a necessity in order to achieve a more rational society and in itself an essential feature of any social order that claims to be both rational and humane. Two reasons support this position. In the first place, rationality is and has to remain an historical conception that changes in accord with changing knowledge that can never be perfect nor complete. This reason leads to the rejection of any and all static utopias. The second line of reasoning is more general. The most rational and humane society possible would, I think, display some degree of oppression and even injustice, as the price paid to attain other values. Indeed, to demand that all human beings devote absolutely all of their energies to eliminating evil and injustice is in itself somehow mean-spirited, twisted, and narrow. To take the demand literally would be a self-defeating return to barbarism because it would mean the end of those portions of scientific and artistic effort that did not serve immediately visible social ends. Just how one should resolve the issue of how much suffering is acceptable for the sake of other values is a question I do not know how to answer or even if it is answerable at all in any general sense, except to remark that one cannot ignore the feelings of those who have to endure the suffering.[1] Hence the debate over these issues would have to continue in the best society that appears conceivable.

The argument of this essay as a whole rests upon a presumed area of considerable agreement about what is painful and that this pain ought to be reduced. It also assumes that modern conditions make it possible to reduce these pains very much further than their present level without sacrificing other human values and indeed enhancing them. But using agreement on the nature of evil by no means forecloses passionate discussion of the good and its relationship to evil.

In turning to the issues of human suffering and intellectual freedom, the first question to ask is whether there is or can be a conflict between the pursuit of truth and the effort to reduce human suffering. Most scientists and scholars today either avoid the issue by taking refuge in their specialties or by accepting the highly doubtful—and of course ultimately unprovable—assumption that in the long run there can be no such conflict, that maximizing the pursuit of truth will eventually reduce human suffering to the minimum.[2] If we take the no longer completely fanciful case of a scientist about to make a discovery whose inevitable consequence would be the annihilation of all life, we would presumably have grounds for forcibly preventing this scientist from continuing his search for truth. Does this illustration show that we have here come up against some irreconcilable conflict of values? I think not, and rather suspect that both the notions of ultimate conflict of values (as in Max Weber) and an ordered hierarchy of values (as in an Aristotelian cosmos) prevent one from understanding correctly the real nature of this contradiction. It is the kind of contradiction we have encountered before between means and ends,

[1] All human societies so far, be it also noted, have paid very little attention to the feelings of those who paid the price for advances in civilization. An awareness of this fact is the strongest point in the notions of participatory democracy.

[2] Unprovable because one would have to acquire all knowledge in order to test it.

where the only available means contains some feature that frustrates the pursuit of the objective. Thus in the hypothetical illustration, one good reason for stopping the research of this scientist would be the argument that the preservation of human life is in itself a basic prerequisite for the pursuit of further truth. Without human beings to make them there can obviously be no further scientific and intellectual discoveries. Whenever we encounter situations in which the pursuit of one value is the indispensable basis for the attainment of another, it makes no sense to speak of a conflict of values or of a hierarchy of values. Incidentally, this is an empirical and factual issue, not a philosophical one nor a matter of definitions. The contradiction between indispensable but at least in some measure self-defeating methods and the results these methods are supposed to attain rests in the situation itself. Other familiar examples that have already come up for discussion have to do with the pursuit of security in international politics, or the humane objectives of a revolution and the cruelties used in their pursuit. As soon as one can demonstrate that the method is not indispensable, that ways exist or can be found to attain these objectives without these costs, the contradiction disappears.

The contradiction between socially desirable beliefs and the truth is an old and familiar one. Though it is sometimes possible to overcome this contradiction, there can be no guarantee that it will always be possible to do so. There is no reason to believe that the truth will always be beneficial to the "good" side in a political and social conflict, to the oppressed, to the blacks, etc. The only reconciliation I can see is that it is generally wiser to know even the most threatening and unpleasant facts in order to minimize their consequences (to the extent that may be possible) and because there is always the prospect that they may become known anyway. One attempted reconciliation is based upon the correct observation that it is impossible to know all truths. To attempt to find out everything leads only to triviality and confusion. Therefore, the argument continues, one should seek only relevant truths, that is, those that contribute to reducing human misery. But there is no guarantee that the relevant truths will in fact always reduce human misery. Furthermore, to limit the search for truth to these pragmatic and political criteria would be stultifying. There are other possible criteria as well, including aesthetic ones. Any rational society would have to allow for more than one criterion and to permit these criteria to be the subject of continual reexamination.

In advance of knowing what the truth is it is impossible to know what the social consequences will be. Even when the truth is more or less adequately known it is impossible to foresee the consequences for more than a very short time. Further knowledge will be necessary to cope with them. That is still another reason for encouraging as much freedom of inquiry as possible.

Taken together, these considerations are, I would suggest, a more than sufficient refutation of the suggestion that the demand for intellectual freedom is nothing more than the reflection of the selfish group interests of a privileged segment of the population. Nevertheless by itself an affirmation of intellectual freedom in general is no adequate solution to these complex and painful problems. We would do well to be on our guard, since ringing affirmations of freedom in other areas of life have very often turned out to be rhetoric that concealed powerful interests in fact opposed to human welfare and human freedom. Welfare and freedom, furthermore, are not necessarily identical. It is time to make the analysis more sociologically specific.

No human society can afford to permit all kinds of human behavior. If it did permit them, it would soon cease to be a society. Can one seriously maintain then that the advocacy of any and all kinds of human behavior is something that society ought to permit? These obvious comments apply just as much to any conceivable rational society in the future—or a less irrational one than those now existing—as it applies to existing and past societies. What sort of behavior would a rational society have to forbid? To this query contemporary radicals have a straightforward answer: it would have to forbid precisely those activities that have come to be the predominant ones of modern Western society. One can summarize them in a phrase: the use of our enormous scientific and technical power for primarily destructive purposes at home and abroad. One radical philosopher, Herbert Marcuse, has had the courage to draw what appears to be the appropriate conclusion.

Radicals should withdraw now their tolerance of these activities and of those who advocate them.[3]

Marcuse's demonstration that at the present time tolerance often does have repressive consequences I regard as indeed brilliant and penetrating. Yet I have come to reject any implication to the effect that radical movements ought to try to prohibit or prevent the advocacy of the views they are attacking. For reasons already partly indicated, radical goals necessarily have a strong liberal and democratic component. Some variant of democracy provides the only prospect of checking tyranny and irrational abuses of authority. Freedom for the expression of basic political and intellectual differences is both socially useful and a value in its own right. To achieve such goals one has to avoid resorting to means that contradict and nullify the objectives. Radicals have a better prospect of attaining these objectives if they insist upon and extend their own right to criticize instead of trying to deprive others of this right.

To withdraw tolerance actually does not mean much—except as an occasional incitement to rowdy behavior which may or may not serve socially useful purposes depending on detailed circumstances—unless one has the power to do so. Then it is liable to be just bad policy. To prohibit political movements and ideas that appear liable to increase human misery requires an educational dictatorship if the movements are already popular. The cure is likely to be as bad as the disease, if not worse, and ineffective to boot.[4] If, on the other hand, these movements are only marginally popular, efforts to stamp them out and prohibit them are liable to make them popular. Martyrdom is what all opposition movements thrive upon, including those with anti-rational and cruel objectives. Certain combinations of historical circumstance, social structure, and cultural tradition, combinations that are still only roughly understood, will make a society succumb readily to these move-

[3] See his "Repressive Tolerance," in Wolff, Moore, and Marcuse, *A Critique of Pure Tolerance*.

[4] The persistence of pre-Soviet and anti-Soviet attitudes among the Russian population despite a half century of intensive propaganda and political control provides some relevant evidence on this point.

ments. Others can give them strong resistance to the point where public opinion takes care of them. It is better to concentrate effort here in doing what one can to remove the causes than in attacking symptoms.

From this point of view the only sensible obligation is that action should have as strong a rational basis as possible, which implies a willingness to argue and discuss. The ultimate test of discussion is results. The radical can and does reply that pleas for discussion and dialogue are often a smokescreen for delays and evasions, during which time people are dying and suffering. How many napalmed children do American liberals have the right to demand as the price for continuing peaceful dissent through orderly channels? How many twisted lives in the black ghettos? To such questions all possible answers are agonizing. The replies come down to highly uncertain estimates about the future and to counterquestions. How likely is it that the radicals in the present situation may produce even greater suffering and disaster, both in their efforts to gain power and in their efforts to put through their policies? The ultimate test of violence is, after all, results too. And which radicals? And what policies? What is the appropriate timespan in passing judgments of this kind? Though these questions are perplexing and indeed terrifying, by wallowing in such emotions we will not get anything except more terror and perplexity. If the situation in American society is as bad as some radicals claim, a straightforward political revolution cannot cure it. For that matter it is not going to get better very rapidly with or without a revolution or semi-revolutionary attempts. A long period of ferment is necessary beforehand, and the worse the situation the longer the ferment of new ideas and efforts to create a new political and social climate.

Let us therefore ask what conditions would have to be present and what obstacles would have to be overcome in any modern society in order to maximize the degree of intellectual freedom. A few moments ago we had occasion to observe that even a quite rational society would have to prohibit many actions, and that it would indeed prohibit many of the destructive actions that are not only commonplace and legal but highly approved in contemporary societies.[5] Accepting then these prohibitions and a strong popular sentiment in their support as part of the situation we are trying to visualize, what other conditions would be necessary in order to permit a maximum of serious and passionate intellectual debate? If it is possible to obtain a moderately satisfactory grasp of what these conditions are, we will be in a better position to note which ones are absent in modern society, and what, if anything, it may be possible to do about it. More succinctly, we are asking what conditions would allow any society to permit full and free discussion of any and all sorts of viewpoints on all subjects. If some of them are unattainable, as I happen to believe to be the case, we want to know why, and what if anything it is possible to do about others in order to approach such a society.

The first condition would be freedom from external threat. For reasons advanced earlier it seems highly unlikely that this condition can exist. On the other hand, there are very substantial variations that can and do exist on this score. A small country in the backwater of international politics may stand the best chance, or perhaps one whose security and independence is actually parasitic on the strength of a great power. It is an unfortunate fact, long ago recognized by Machiavelli, that attractive political moralities are frequently dependent on the unattractive moralities of others. Turning to internal matters, such a society would have to be blessed with a general population that was emotionally very secure, rational, and with a very high level of education that gave it distinguished capacities of judgment and discrimination. Though not easy to attain, this objective does not seem out of the question. Furthermore there would have to be at least some rough equality among the various contestants in regard to the social and economic pressures they could exert formally and informally on behalf of

[5] Such prohibitions would be the basis of freedom and rationality in the same way that the prohibition of murder is the basis of security in orderly and peaceful communities now. In fact, the relationship would have to be very similar in that the mass of the population felt neither need nor compulsion to engage in the destructive behavior that characterizes modern industrial society. Laws against murder are of but marginal use in communities so torn by strife that killing becomes a commonplace of daily life.

other views. There could not, in other words, be a very powerful establishment with *de facto* control over the economy, access to education and the content of education, the channels of public communication. No complex society has existed for any length of time without such an establishment, even if some, such as the English, have been moderately open. It is uncertain whether any large society could exist without such an establishment. As even the English example suggests, the less obtrusive and oppressive the machinery of government, the more effective have to be informal social controls. If these informal controls amount to a diffuse censorship of ideas among the populace at large, as they generally do, there is a very slight prospect of serious debate and difference in the population as a whole, though it could exist in elite circles. On the other hand, if, as postulated above, the population were sufficiently educated, confident and secure in its social institutions and stock of ideas, and also had a touch of intellectual curiosity and daring, there is at least the possibility that it might tolerate continuous critical reexamination of its basic premises.

In other areas there would probably have to be some degree of at least informal control over intellectual innovations. No society could tolerate an endless sequence of rapid and fundamental changes. Furthermore, in a society such as we are trying to visualize, the formal and informal priorities of scientific and technical research would be very different from those in modern Western society. For these reasons alone it seems quite clear that absolute intellectual freedom is incompatible not just with utopia but even with a moderately decent society. Hence the issues come down not to the presence or absence of limitations, but to what the limitations are and through what persons and social mechanisms they take effect.

Any conceivable society, it appears, including one that had reduced the major sources of human misery to a minimum, would be likely to encounter the problem of dangerous thoughts. The traditional rationalist assumptions in effect reject this conclusion. According to this tradition, if human beings are not corrupted or perverted by evil institutions and if discussion is full and free, arguments and evidence will somehow always turn up in the end that will have the socially desirable results that the rationalists seek. As pointed out earlier in this chapter there is no reason to make such an optimistic assumption. The most one can claim is that it is better to know unpleasant facts that are relevant to one's purposes because otherwise one will come to grief sooner or later anyhow. If there is such a thing as racial differences in intelligence, or if the methods used to raise the intellectual capacities of black slum children are not working for any reason whatever, it is better to know this fact from the standpoint of both intellectual honesty and decent social policy.

A rational society would face up to dangerous thoughts. It would not taboo or prohibit their investigation. These considerations, though valid, still do not get to the sociological roots of the problem. The questions asked, the conceptual tools used, the problems emphasized, and the general allocation of scarce intellectual resources, all reflect in large measure the interests and conceptions of the dominant groups in the society. At any given moment in any specific society scientists and scholars consider only a tiny fraction of the problems that could be considered. There are huge areas of unthinkable thought. Some thoughts are unthinkable because the stock of accumulated knowledge and technique is insufficient even for perceiving the problem. In other areas the problems may be perceived but their investigation deemed not worthwhile in terms of the intellectual priorities that derive from the existing structure of knowledge. Or their investigation is not deemed rewarding for more material reasons. There is no such thing as pure freedom of research now. Nor could there be in any society, including the most rational one.

Finally, for free discussion to mean more than disagreeable noise the participants have to possess both technical and more general intellectual competence. There is no such thing as a "right" to one's own opinions. I have no right to believe that 2 plus 2 = 5. There is no more than a general right to correct and well-grounded opinions. Indeed, "right" is an inexact term. We should speak only of warrants and grounds for opinions. An individual may have the best grounds for certain opinions and feelings about his own situation because he is the one with the most opportunity for experience about this situation. In colloquial language he is the one who can really know where the shoe pinches. But even these feelings can be full of illusions and misconceptions. What husband or wife accurately perceives the meaning of everything said and done in relation to the other marital partner? About wider social and intellectual issues it is impossible for every individual to be competent and informed in all areas.

Does this impossibility mean that all serious decisions have to be turned over to presumed experts? There are, I hold, good reasons for rejecting this conclusion, or at least for asserting that it is not inevitable. We often hear that with the modern explosion of knowledge it has become impossible to know everything. That is of course true. But that does not mean that everything is worth knowing, that intelligent people could not come to agreement about criteria that distinguish trivial from valuable knowledge. In practice, distinctions take effect. What is necessary is that they be subject to rational and continuous evaluation. Furthermore, I doubt that the basic intellectual issues in the natural and social sciences and the humanities are beyond the grasp of ordinary educated people. In fact this is what an ordinary liberal education is supposed to impart but rarely does. A liberal education should impart considerably more because a person who knew only the principles of those fields of knowledge that now have them, and the unresolved arguments about whether such principles are either desirable or possible in other fields, would have no more than a very superficial education, indeed a highly deceptive one that could make him or her into a dangerously pretentious barbarian. Granting these difficulties and the extreme improbability of an educational system that could turn out people with discriminating judgment if not highly specialized technical competence in more than one field of knowledge, I still suspect that it would be possible if the society chose to direct its efforts in that direction. In such a society the level of judgment would be sufficiently high to exercise a check upon sheer expertise. Nothing of this sort is likely to happen, however, until and unless modern culture overcomes its present fragmentation. That prospect is remote.

The discussion has turned up two obstacles to maximum intellectual liberty that could perhaps be considered historically contingent ones. One of these is a very unequal distribution of access to and command over natural and social resources, or in less precise but blunter language, wealth and power. The other derives from the recurring imperatives of international politics. To call them historically contingent does not imply that these obstacles would be easy to overcome. Such is very far from the case. It does indicate that these obstacles and limitations may not be inherent in the nature of intellectual inquiry itself or in the imperatives of any form of social living among human beings. Two other obstacles, I suggest, are of this latter sort. One is the general problem of allocating limited intellectual resources among a variety of purposes, a situation that makes some sort of formal or informal controls inevitable. The second derives from the presumed necessity for the existence of strong moral sentiments in any human society, the impossibility of any purely rationalist and calculated morality that appealed for its sanctions to no more than probable consequences of different kinds of action. The capacity for feeling horror at some kinds of behavior seems to be a necessity for human civilization. This type of moral obstacle to complete intellectual freedom presents the most intriguing problems of all. One should not, however, press the distinction between historically contingent and more essential obstacles too strongly, because advances in knowledge can change the meaning of these categories.

Thus the persecution of heresy is nothing more than an especially acute and painful form of the limitation on intellectual freedom that every human society has imposed, and seems likely to impose, as the price human beings have to pay in order to live together. But when we look at the issue from this perspective we can also see an equally significant trend at work, the attempt to create what a modern political scientist would be likely to call a system of legitimate opposition.

Logically that is something which ought not to exist: the authority to challenge authority. It is, I would venture to say, the essence of liberalism. There has been a tendency to identify this essence much too closely with the contributions of the bourgeoisie and of capitalism, a tendency which gives a very false perspective upon contemporary problems. Important though the "bourgeois" contribution has been, it is very far from the only one. Without taking too seriously Tacitus's remarks about the German tribes or the remarks of nineteenth-century romantic Westerners and their native imitators about Hindu society as congeries of "little republics," it is possible to extend very widely through time and space the range of evidence for a tendency to limit authority through some form of organized opposition.

This tendency has worked itself out under a very wide variety of conditions: the city states of Greece and Rome, the very different world of European feudalism, and then again in more recent times accompanying and following the decline of absolute monarchies. A very large portion of the impulse has been aristocratic. Demands for parliamentary control over the levying of taxes began to take effect in the Middle Ages in connection with the wars of the English king with France. Likewise in the late Middle Ages the right to criticize authority received a powerful impetus from the demand by members of parliament to be able to talk freely among themselves and to have a collective speaker. All this was part of a much wider historical transformation whose significance it is easy to forget. To move from assassination, execution, or their milder forms—impeachment and bills of attainder—as a way of changing leaders and policies, to political parties and more or less free discussion was no easy and simple task. Revolutionary violence played its part in this process. On the other hand, the movement towards legitimate opposition was an attempt to find ways of settling disputes without resort to violence, without roasting men for their opinions, without tearing human society apart. The fact that such efforts go back at least twenty-five centuries in time, that they recur under very widely differing historical circumstances, indicates that liberal theory and practice meet some form of felt necessity quite independent of capitalism or industrialism, though certainly the demand has existed there too. To claim that the tendency is pan-human or an irrepressible aspect of our biological equipment would be mistaken, there is only too much evidence that human beings can be conditioned to accept oppression. From this comparative historical perspective the liberal impulse appears mainly as an attempt to correct abuses, though there is also a current of intellectual efforts to construct a society where the abuses are less likely to occur. Only if one can believe that it is possible to construct a society completely free of abuses, or a permanently effective system of oppression, can one bring oneself to believe that the liberal impulse is historically obsolete.

To the extent that this analysis is correct we are in a better position to assess the current situation in modern liberal democratic societies. Since the next two chapters address themselves to these issues, I will confine the discussion here to certain general matters and problems that have to do mainly with intellectual life. Whatever the social and historical prerequisites may be for liberal democratic societies, it is obvious that these conditions do not flourish in any leading state (not to mention client states) of what is called with euphemistic arrogance the free world. On the other hand, liberal societies are the only ones that in their official doctrines explicitly reject persecution for holding or advocating unpopular ideas, even if their practice very often falls far short of this ideal.[6] They are also the only societies that have acquired explicit institutional arrangements for changing and criticizing prevailing orthodoxies, that is, for giving change the aura of propriety and legitimacy. Indeed, these two related characteristics are precisely what distinguish liberal polities and societies from others. We often judge the extent to which any society is actually liberal—for many claim to be such that are not—by the extent to which it does in practice allow the open expression of dissent and the effectiveness of dissent in bringing about changes in the workings and structure of the social mechanism. To me this seems very reasonable. As one skeptical of social perfection I hold that societies should be judged by how much and about what it is possible to complain, and whether the complaints do any good. A society without visible complaints should automatically be an object of the gravest suspi-

---

[6] In revolutionary and post-revolutionary dictatorships such institutions are window-dressing modifications of liberal arrangements.

cion. Either its population is obtuse or its rulers cruel tyrants, or both.[7]

In broad outline the main social devices for getting around these obstacles and for meeting the contrary pulls between the search for freedom and innovation and the requirements of social stability have taken the form of efforts by various types of thinkers to wall themselves off from the rest of the social order, to obtain special dispensations and privileges within this order. Universities, professional associations, and the artist's bohemia with its claim of artistic license and a special code to govern the artist's behavior, are the main manifestations of this tendency. They differ from priestly castes and occupational guilds of earlier ages in their explicit effort to make innovation possible. To anyone with strong democratic, perhaps populist (though not necessarily socialist) convictions, these arrangements exude a disagreeable odor of elitism and hypocrisy. Where elitism is based on demonstrable differences in the capacity of different individuals to meet acceptable social needs it is not difficult to defend. One can also defend special privilege for the genius who meets no visible social need, and especially the one who creates new needs or attacks outworn ones. Hypocrisy is another matter, although if it ceased to exist, social analysts would lose a major clue to understanding the workings of human society. The most one can say in its defense is that it is often an unavoidable social technique for patching over irreconcilable social and psychological imperatives. Unavoidable hypocrisy we might agree to call make-believe.

Among the institutions just mentioned I shall limit myself to some comments on the university. One reason for this limitation is that among contemporary social arrangements the modern Western university is the main one that has endeavored to make intellectual criticism and innovation a legitimate and regular aspect of the prevailing social order. To institutionalize heresy is at bottom probably an impossible task because it means making heresy respectable, at

[7] In the 1950's the absence of complaints seemed to its critics the most disturbing symptom in American society. By the end of the next decade, a diagnosis in terms of conformity and lack of opposition would have appeared absurd.

which point it ceases to be heresy. Nevertheless the effort is an interesting one about which I happen to know something from personal experience. Certainly the university displays a great deal of elitism, hypocrisy, and make-believe. But where do these features come from? How are they related to the central tasks of a university? Where do the justifiable and unjustifiable aspects begin and end?

A great many of the university's present and severe difficulties arise from the fact that it has no agreed-upon ideals, no established purpose, a reflection of wider processes of disintegration in Western culture as a whole. Instead it has several goals and purposes that are in conflict with one another. The old liberal ideal of a disinterested pursuit of truth and beauty remains a very powerful one, at the larger private universities still the predominant one among the faculty and, more recently, among many gifted students. Another purpose is that of service to the nation and to the community, an objective that comes increasingly into conflict with the preceding one as American domestic and foreign policy departs from liberal ideals. Still a third goal is to train the young in certain general skills and in that more intangible quality known as "character," which in practice amounts to an enthusiastic acceptance of the status quo. Finally, there is the less openly acknowledged purpose of serving as a social mixing bowl that enables the more energetic and capable students from plebeian backgrounds to acquire both useful skills and a touch of social polish and hence move a few rungs up the social ladder. The present crisis in the universities is a struggle over these goals, in which the radical students are attacking all of the preceding goals and seeking to replace them with a much stronger emphasis on a new goal of service to the people and miscellaneous radical social objectives. They can count on considerable support from many other students who feel a general malaise about the gap between ideals and realities in the United States, a gap that has always been present in considerable degree, but about which they are forced by the draft and a vicious war to reach an immediate personal decision.

Among these purposes the only one that receives explicit acknowledgment and acceptance from those universities that enjoy the greatest prestige is the disinterested pursuit of truth and beauty. Though the consequences of such a pursuit cannot be altogether disinterested, a topic sufficiently discussed above, it would be an utterly fatal error to dismiss this goal as a total impossibility and to treat its place in modern university life as sheer rhetoric. There is such a thing as pursuing an intellectual quest irrespective of the consequences, of changing one's own mind, and as may actually happen more often, that of other people—especially good students —with what one finds. Nor should we underestimate the extent to which these activities do actually take place in a good university. They are what a university is set up to do, and to a surprising extent they exist. As one who holds that these pursuits are in themselves the finest flower of human civilization I also believe that they should be the primary goal of university life, though I very much doubt that such will be the consequence of the crisis through which the universities and the society in which they are embedded are passing.

Because the ideal is an impossible one to realize in a pure form within society as it exists, or in any form of society that seems likely to emerge for a long time to come, the whole enterprise does of course display considerable make-believe and even hypocrisy which readily corrupts the objectives. To see these aspects requires no great powers of penetration, and I shall not elaborate upon familiar details. It is impossible to isolate the university from the surrounding society in order to make it a complete island of freedom for alternate contemplation and hard work. It is impossible to select students purely on the basis of their individual capacity and desire for a brief period of experimental participation in such a life. It is impossible for fallible human mortals to seek truth and beauty with the passion they require and deserve and still maintain the conviction that a person who thinks and acts differently is neither a knave nor a fool.[8] How impossible? How much make-believe has to be built into the system? Let us look more closely at these asserted impossibilities.

[8] The assumption that such is the case is a necessary prerequisite for reasoned discourse. Academic appointment procedures supposedly ensure that such will be the case. But they are not infallible.

The impossibility of combining passion and detachment has its psychological and its social side. To make this combination anywhere near possible the university has to separate itself off from the surrounding society at the very least to the point where vindictive voices from the outside do not mean the loss of a job for outspoken faculty members or equivalent penalties for students in similar situations. There is more to this necessity than the simple matter of intimidation, even though intimidation is very important, especially in its more subtle and less blatant forms. Careerist ambition is at least as great a source of self-deception as fear. What makes possible both passion and willingness to listen to others is some degree of separation from real life, some protection from immediate responsibility for thought and action.

This issue is a delicate and complex one. If the university were really able to separate itself off from the surrounding society to the point where it felt no impact from the great issues of the day, it would be even more sterile than it actually is. That prospect, however, is most improbable. On the other hand, there is a greatly inflated mythology about the significance of practical and concrete experience. Active involvement in social causes is very often an excuse to hide one's head in the sand of small decisions and thereby evade facing the central issues. Sheer activism is merely a narcotic. That is true all across the political spectrum. Somewhere between the much abused conception of the ivory tower and the overly praised virtue of commitment there is an optimum point of detachment and separation from the world. It is the point at which the deception of oneself and others from hope and fear is at a minimum. It exists wherever there are good grounds for believing that a colleague's arguments in the classroom are not really dangerous to humanity because they are put forth not for action, at least not for immediate action, but for tentative discussion and scrutiny. I confess that I am unable to specify it more closely than that. This experimental and slightly remote character of academic life is, I think, part of the price it is necessary to pay in order to have any serious and free intellectual life at all. Does this aspect change in a new age when professors depart in droves to take high policy positions with the government? There are good reasons for thinking that it changes rather less than seems to be the case on the surface. By and large, government officials take and buy the advice they want, in their struggles with each other and segments of the general public. Therefore a professor does not become a danger to humanity, or the man whose ideas may preserve Western civilization (both *may* amount to the same thing) by getting on an airplane to Washington. The reason to be alarmed is not that X and Y now have the government's ear. The reason to be alarmed is that there is a powerful demand for such advice.

The difficulty of combining passion with detachment arises most acutely from the issue of whether or not the university, presumably committed to the free exchange of ideas through rational discourse, should or should not appoint to its faculty someone firmly committed to a philosophy strongly opposed to freedom of speech. This is one of those situations where circumstances greatly alter cases, and where in actual practice a great deal depends on estimates of the general intelligence of the individual under consideration as well as whether the commitment is merely a formal one, indicated by membership in a political party, or whether it runs much deeper than that. Nevertheless the situation is worth discussing in general terms because of the issues it brings to the surface. Although there are powerful arguments against granting such a person membership in the community of scholars, on balance I think that the university should accept such persons.[9]

There are two reasons for refusing to accept them. In the first place, a scholar's role is not that of an advocate such as, for example, a trial lawyer. If a defense lawyer is suddenly surprised by a piece of evidence or an argument turned up by the prosecution, he is never supposed to say, "My, I had never thought of that! It's a good point and my client must be guilty." On the other hand, that is exactly what an intellectually honest scholar is supposed to do under such circumstances. If he is intellectually incapable of doing this or under some external constraint that prevents him from so

[9] Though we come to opposite conclusions, I have received much help in discussing this issue with Robert Paul Wolff. For his view see, *The Ideal of the University* (Boston, 1969), 129. In part of what follows I reproduce to the best of my recollection points he made in our conversations.

doing, he is *ipso facto* unable to fulfill the role of scientist or scholar. Presumably this argument would serve to bar Catholic scholars (at least from some areas of inquiry) as well as communists and fascists. In the second place, heterodox opinions do not have intellectual merit simply because they are heterodox. There exists, after all, a reasonably clear procedure for evaluating opinions on the basis of logic and evidence. No department in the natural sciences would feel under obligation to appoint someone who believed that the earth was flat simply because there might be something to this hypothesis. In order to be "well rounded," as the banal phrase goes, a university department does not have to present a full catalogue of human absurdities.

On the other hand, in the study of human affairs there is nothing like the extent of agreement prevailing in the physical sciences about theories or even the proper way to evaluate them. The previous generation's certainties have a way of turning into today's absurdities, while it would be a bold prophet who could declare that none of today's absurdities will be tomorrow's platitudes. In my own judgment a great deal of this waffling about is both foolish and unnecessary. But it would be disastrous to try to prevent it by some form of *fiat;* there are enough irrational elements in the formation of sound professional opinion already. And for that matter there is a great deal more fluctuation in the natural sciences than is quite commonly supposed. Furthermore, the challenge to orthodoxy is built into the whole historical process. If there were some way of determining that certain types of challenges, e.g. those from the "right" were always "bad" and those from the "left" always "good"—or that "extreme" ideas were always "bad" and "moderate" ideas always "good"—there would be grounds for promoting certain political and philosophical currents and opposing or even prohibiting others. Over short periods of time, a generation or so, such knowledge is available in rather rough-and-ready form, in the sense of some general awareness of what ideas and policies are likely to contribute to human misery and which ones show promise of diminishing it. All societies set limits upon the pursuit of this form of knowledge even if, consciously or not, only to make other people do the suffering. But that is exactly the point:

the knowledge is always rough-and-ready and distorted by passion and partisanship. Now the essence of the rational outlook is that no idea is above and beyond critical examination.

This perpetual re-examination is the principal task of the community of scholars, which is not a claim that they perform it in the manner they should. It is impossible to carry on this process without re-examiners who have not only good minds but also some emotional charge behind their intellectual processes. A liberal argument that cannot stand up before a radical onslaught is not worth having and vice versa; neither of them are worth having if they cannot stand up to a fascist critique. The fascist viewpoint has to be rejected on objective grounds, and not simply refused a hearing. Presumably the only person who could present these grounds effectively is someone who finds them convincing. Unless one can demonstrate in a thoroughly objective manner that the grounds for conviction are mistaken, the most obnoxious and dangerous convictions do, I think, deserve a critical hearing within the somewhat special situation of a university.

Indeed one could go further. Because in practice there will always be strong pressures in favor of the prevailing political and social orthodoxies, a university that tries to live up to its rhetoric about intellectual freedom has a special obligation to seek out talented spokesmen for whatever ideas are currently repressed. The obligation applies both to the left and to the right of whatever portion of the political spectrum happens to be respectable. There is at the same time an obligation that rests upon the spokesman for non-liberal and anti-liberal doctrines, and which leads to an obvious contradiction. By accepting membership in the scholarly community the spokesman for anti-liberal doctrines undertakes the obligation to refrain from using anything except purely intellectual weapons to advance his viewpoint. The freedom to advance his or her own viewpoint depends upon actively upholding the corresponding freedom of his intellectual opponents. Such a professor cannot, for example, stir up students to disrupt the classes of those who are intellectual opponents. Instead there would be an obligation to oppose such disruptions. (Presumably outside the university such a person takes his or her chances with the law, along with everyone else.) Quite clearly this obligation breaks the link between thought and action, a link that is especially important among the adherents to anti-liberal doctrines.

Under prevailing conditions this obligation to play within the rules of the game works obvious injustices upon leftist radicals. A "liberal" professor can go to Washington and collaborate with the Pentagon or some other agency on a murderous undertaking and remain perfectly within the rules of the game. On the other hand, students or faculty members who protest such actions in any way that interferes with the freedom of movement of the collaborator with the Pentagon run the risk of severe disciplinary penalties. That is the basic reason for the disenchantment with liberalism in general, for the widespread belief that it has become a hypocritical mask for violence. The only ways in which the scales could be made even would be through a corresponding limitation on the liberals' freedom to act in accordance with their beliefs, or a change in the liberals' general conception of the world to the point where they develop a tacit but effective code that precludes collaboration with repressive government policies or agencies. Since there is likely to be sharp disagreement about who and what actually are repressive for a long time to come, the problem will almost certainly remain insoluble for the foreseeable future. Whether this form of conflict may eventually tear liberal society apart, and whether there are good grounds for holding that it either will or should come apart, are larger issues whose consideration I will defer to the next chapter.

Instead I will return to what appears to me a very strong practical reason for allowing adherents of anti-liberal doctrines to become members of the community of scholars, and indeed for making an effort to recruit some talented ones. The mere fact that a person claims to be willing to change his mind in the face of contrary evidence is no guarantee that he will be able to do so.[10] Even less does the fact that a scholar formally adheres to a "liberal" standpoint guarantee the intellectual flexibility that is part of

[10] From this point on I shall not try to avoid the male chauvinism that is built into the language: an impersonal "he" will automatically mean "he or she."

commencement-day rhetoric. In fact practically everybody claims to have this virtue, no matter what his point of view. Very intelligent people are even more reluctant to admit that they lack the ability to change their minds, or that they have lost this ability, than they are willing to admit they lack a sense of humor. As far as I can see, there is really no sure way of determining this absence of intellectual integrity in advance that does not amount to a blanket proscription of ideas. If indeed there were some clear and unambiguous test of both intellectual competence and integrity of this sort, to be given, let us say on an annual basis as a condition for keeping one's job, how many of us would be able to pass it?

The same tensions between commitment and detachment, between being part of the society and distinct from it, arise in connection with that cherished value: freedom of research. Clearly that is not an absolute value. If some wealthy eccentric should offer to provide funds for a research program on how to make and plant bombs to blow up libraries and laboratories, no university administration or faculty would accept the grant. Nor is it likely that members of the faculty would rise to make ringing speeches about freedom of research in order to defend such a grant. Yet they have made such speeches on many a campus in defense of military research which has undoubtedly been responsible for the death of thousands of innocent victims. Evidently it is not the prospect that research will have destructive consequences that necessarily leads those in a university to override the value of freedom of research. The inevitable limitations of resources, both human ones and material ones, also serve to constrain freedom of choice in determining what can be investigated and what cannot. There is still another and closely related constraint: the prevailing judgment in a given field of inquiry as to what problems are significant or interesting and which ones are not. For example, no mathematician is likely to receive a huge grant to compute the value of pi to several hundred further decimal places. The problem is just not regarded as significant. Judgments of significance and interest in turn arise out of a combination of both past traditions and the state of knowledge in a field, or purely intellectual factors which have their own autonomous momentum, and social, economic, and political factors that impinge upon an investigator from the larger society.

These issues have gained salience in recent times through radical attacks on the "myth of university neutrality" and the demand for "relevance." The cry of relevance in turn becomes a cover for all sorts of historical and cultural provincialism and the demands of special interest groups. The cry for relevance becomes just one more obstacle to the serious consideration of fundamental issues, a mirror image of the demand that universities become service stations for the status quo. In the face of such demands the university is paralyzed, because its own myths lead to the rejection of any conception of a coherent intellectual strategy, any general grounds that would enable academics to say, for example, that knowledge about human heredity is more important than information about some fourth-rate political scribbler.

The curriculum thus becomes more and more of a cafeteria. Since it is impossible to claim that it represents the outcome of any defensible and rational intellectual process, any sensible use of resources, academics are forced to waste time either discussing the curriculum again and again, or else raising the absence of strategy to a virtue. To have no way of distinguishing significance from triviality is scarcely a proud badge for professional thinkers. In theory it amounts to conceding the right of the strongest. In practice it means that the university sells its services to the highest bidder and makes concessions to those who kick it the hardest.

Somewhere down that road lies death with dishonor. To be sure, a university can still "exist." It can continue to exist by becoming nothing more than a service agency for the status quo, stifling all critical voices. Conceivably a university could even become a service station for revolution, though that is much more doubtful. So far universities have only been service stations for revolutionary regimes after they have themselves become new forms of status quo. Nevertheless, a university that exists only as a service station for *either* the status quo or the revolution has ceased to be a place where people can think freely, where critical rationality can exist at all. A university where a professor cannot on some occasions and with some real effect say "the people be damned" is not worth having. Nor does a university deserve its name where it is impossible to make similar and effective observations about the exalted of the world.

These remarks imply that there has hardly ever been anything that really deserved to be called a university, a position with which I see no reason to quarrel. It is something to strive for, not celebrate. A rational academic system would be one that admitted those and only those who demonstrated intellectual capacity and motivation. By this criterion, degree-giving country clubs would go out of business. A sensible system of higher education would be much more elitist and rather less snobbish than what exists. It would be better to enable those who are gifted to make the most of their gifts. In so doing it is helpful to let them mix with primarily, though not exclusively, with other gifted students instead of simultaneously holding them back and allowing them to develop delusions of grandeur (mixed nowadays with guilt feelings) because they can easily perform better than their age mates.

Intellectual qualities of course are not merely a matter of individual endowment. They are also a product of the entire social and cultural environment in which a young person has grown up. Or perhaps more accurately the stultification of these qualities in a way that does tragically permanent damage to the individual comes about from growing up in certain types of environments—not all of them, incidentally, lower-class and Afro-American. Until quite recently the very rich have been quite successful in enforcing and transmitting their own brand of brutal stupidity. About all this the university can do nothing, at least not in the short run. Remedial programs to enable youngsters to overcome handicaps due to background are likely to work in only a limited number of cases where motivation remains high and basic aptitudes have not been destroyed. For the young person who has been unable to learn what self-discipline means because self-discipline makes no sense in such a life, such programs come too late to make a difference. That is just as true of the spoiled rich brat as the slum child. Thus universities are bound to reflect the injustices of the surrounding society. It is these injustices that require attack rather than their reflections and symptoms. At the same time if the university reflects only too perfectly the injustices of the surrounding society, or even intensifies them by concealing their existence from the student body through the failure to challenge accepted myths, it belies its own liberal justifications and forgets the moral right to those privileges claimed on this basis.

From this general assessment there follow certain obligations for the academic intellectual. The first is to try to uncover and expose the roots of violence and the threats to human freedom that derive from the prevailing social order. Under present and foreseeable circumstances in the United States this conception of his obligation places the critical rationalist in sharp opposition to official liberalism as expressed by political leaders, including those in the left wing of the Democratic party. The task of critical exposure of course runs much wider and deeper than concern with the ephemera of daily politics. Even more broadly conceived it is not everyone's job. But it is a crucial one, and shared with certain radicals. At the same time, the academic intellectual has the equal obligation to avoid capitulation to the intellectual provincialism of the oppressed and the pseudo-oppressed. In social action, which is much less part of the academic intellectual's *métier* but not necessarily excluded from it, there is an obligation to work for the removal of institutions and abuses that threaten to overwhelm what there is of an open society, and to do what is possible to establish such a society.

More concretely, with respect to the everyday life of existing universities this position implies an awareness that the pursuit of knowledge unavoidably has political consequences. It is impossible to foresee many of these, especially as some of the most important ones may well lie in a distant future. Nevertheless, professional thinkers should see to it that these consequences are as far as possible humane and constructive ones, that they reduce rather than increase the amount of misery and cruelty at large in this world. What are humane and constructive purposes change with historical circumstances, and from this standpoint remain forever open for redefinition. In discussing both the means to attain them and the ends themselves, anyone who adopts this stand will realize that the choices are seldom unequivocal and easy, that all of them may involve serious costs.

The most difficult intellectual tasks, therefore, will often be to distinguish between serious argument and specious rationalization. Adherence to this view of the world implies a large measure of courtesy and detachment that nevertheless stops short of both blandness and intellectual irresponsibility. Finally, the conception of humane and constructive purposes does not only include working for the removal of specific evils and abuses, even if their stench reaches to the heavens. Trying to be humane also includes giving a large place to the search for truth that widens human horizons in time and space and for the beauty that enriches it. These too are political conceptions, for they are part of what makes life worth living. Here too there is an obligation to be aware of the cost, to realize that the costs are not readily measurable—perhaps in a deeper sense not measurable at all, since those who pay them may use a different moral and intellectual currency—and hence to make a serious effort to see that the obvious material costs do not fall upon those least able to pay.

This conception presupposes for its full development a form of society that has never existed. Meanwhile attempts to approximate it, it is often asserted, are passing from the historical stage. Perhaps that is so. Are critical rationalists like intelligent pagans in the last phase of classical civilization? Probably with some violence to the historical facts, in moments of relaxed musing one can imagine a pagan thinker sufficiently intelligent and humane to perceive that the Roman Empire was cruel and corrupt, that its rationale was nonsense which no intelligent person could take seriously any longer. If this pagan had a slightly sensitive conscience, he might be uncomfortably aware that the soldiers on distant ramparts, whose plundering he criticized, still somehow indirectly supported not only his own privileges and right of detached contemplation but also the liberties of those who more radically attacked the social order, as in fact Symmachus taunted the Christians. If he were curious too, he would of course make every effort to gain a sympathetic yet critical understanding of the new forces of ferment and change in his world, the Christians and the myriad sects with whom they competed and quarreled. And if he were at all successful in his effort at understanding, he might gain at least some dim sense that for a long time to come these new forces could only create something much worse: that out of the rhetoric of brotherhood there could easily come bloodshed, chaos, heresy, persecution, the Crusades, and the Inquisition. . . .

Someone who reflects along these lines soon comes to realize that human civilization has never been arranged mainly for the benefit of the doubters and the skeptics. A moderately thoughtful person will not waste much time in self-pity on that score. The world is too full of terror and wonder, which cry out for the effort at disciplined understanding; there is just too much work to be done for indulgence in this form of luxury. The critic should also be modest enough to realize that the role of doubter and skeptic is not the only one in the human drama. Therefore such a person will not try to force this role upon those unsuited to taking it.

At the same time he, and nowadays fortunately she, will take due pride in this role so long as it remains at all a possible one. Just as they do not force this role upon others, and respect those who act in very different ways on behalf of humane ideals, they will insist on respect for their own role, for the freedom to choose it, and resist with whatever force and courage they can command any attempt to deprive them of the right to take it. They will not be afraid to call in question the inevitable, which, in the words of C. Vann Woodward, needs all the opposition it can get because it is usually unpleasant. And, one may add, the inevitable is seldom what anybody expected.

V

Of Predatory Democracy: the USA

What is wrong with American society? The question has a banal ring and a set of familiar answers. Scarcely a week goes by without some pundit raising and answering the question. It is tempting to dismiss it in the manner of those to the left of platitudinous respectability, to turn it into the assertion, "What's wrong *is* American society; its mere existence is the greatest disaster of the twentieth century. It is *the* cause of human misery in our time." That is probably the one thesis upon which all contemporary Western radicals (and of course many Russian and even more Chinese ones) would readily agree. To many others such a claim generally looks like a piece of silly rhetoric, a shibboleth in the literal sense of a cultish phrase by which true believers recognize one another and exclude the nonbelievers. But this dismissal has become less and less easy under the pressure of events. The complacent myth that American society is one where competing pressure groups manage through the democratic process to resolve in a peaceful fashion the social problems of advanced industrial society now stands exposed as a myth. Those who hold to it are clearly on the defensive, while radical ideas have attained a certain degree of modish respectability. Indeed, there is a considerable danger that one myth may simply be replaced by another, as has happened so often before.

Since myths about one's own society serve to provide an orientation towards the world without which human beings would become helpless and even insane gibbering idiots (here again in the old, literal sense of idiot as a person with a purely private, unshared, and unsanctioned conception of his physical and social surroundings), it is not a very promising task to try to distinguish myth from reality, to try to penetrate beyond the wishful thinking of both critics and defenders of the status quo to the actual situation and its real possibilities for change. Nevertheless the task is unavoidable and, I hold, the central obligation, though certainly not the sole one, of the professional student of human affairs.

It will be best to begin by setting down very briefly those points in the radical critique that have been established with what I take to be a high degree of probability. First of all, the New Deal did not constitute a successful resolution of the problems of advanced capitalist society within the democratic framework.[1] The Second World War, not the New Deal, pulled the United States out of the depression. Secondly, since that time military expenditures have played a crucial role in sustaining aggregate demand, thereby preventing a major depression—at least up until 1971. As far as I can ascertain, there is not much dispute between liberal and radical economists on the fact of this connection, though the degree of its importance is not easy to measure exactly. Rather the dispute turns upon the issue of whether or not the connection is a necessary one.[2] As a third point that hardly needs belaboring, American military force has for some time been used to support reactionary regimes in the economically backward parts of the globe. Indeed, for the past decade the main thrust of American foreign policy has been counter-revolutionary.[3] Whether this counter-revolutionary foreign policy reflects an economic imperative appears to me rather more doubtful, a point to be discussed more fully in a moment. Be that as it may, there is no doubt that the United States has since the Second World War become vastly more dependent on foreign sources of raw materials in order to support its current levels of production and consumption. The whole material paraphernalia of the consumers' society from automobiles through refrigerators to

[1] On this point see especially the work of an historian whom I would certainly not consider radical: Ellis W. Hawley, *The New Deal and the Problem of Monopoly* (Princeton and London, 1966).

[2] For the views of a liberal economist see Alvin H. Hansen, *The Postwar American Economy* (New York, 1964).

[3] Whether revolutions could reduce suffering is another issue, discussed in the next chapter.

tin cans now means that the United States is the greatest gobbler of raw materials of any state on the globe.[4]

While American foreign policy has been primarily counter-revolutionary, domestic policy according to the perception of radicals has been essentially one of sops and tokenism with no small overtones of police repression. Hence their general image of America is one of a society that devotes its overwhelming resources primarily to destructive purposes while scattering no more than a handful of them among its own poor. These in turn appear as a large and increasing segment of the population, many of them with dark skins. In this image of the domestic situation there is more than sufficient truth to be very disturbing for anyone who holds that the reduction of human suffering rather than its increase is the proper goal of human society. On the other hand, there are also reasons to believe that in its image of the American domestic scene the radical indictment begins to display a significant element of rhetorical exaggeration. To separate truth from polemical rhetoric merely on this aspect alone would require several books much larger than this one—with results that are problematic, given the tenacity of human convictions. Here as elsewhere I can do no more than draw attention to some of the main considerations.

Let us begin with some of the more obviously tenable aspects of the indictment. More than a century after the Civil War the democratic promise of judging men and women upon their merits instead of upon the color of their skin remains one whose general fulfillment remains perpetually postponed. Though there are cogent arguments to the effect that the plight of urban blacks is essentially an economic one rather than a racial one, that nothing very much in their situation could be expected to change overnight if by some miracle their skins suddenly turned white or that

[4] See in addition to Gabriel Kolko, *The Roots of American Foreign Policy* (Boston, 1969); Harry Magdoff, *The Age of Imperialism* (New York and London, 1969); and Paul R. Ehrlich and Anne H. Ehrlich, *Population, Resources, Environment* (San Francisco, 1970). Though there are important differences in their views, to be discussed later, both Kolko and Magdoff are radical scholars. The Ehrlichs are biologists whom it would be hard to place under this rubric.

of the whites turned black and race prejudice disappeared,[5] the establishment of this point does not take us very far. It is necessary to remember how their economic situation became what it is and the part that racial oppression and prejudice have played in this long history. That the corporate elite derives any benefits from this state of affairs seems to me hardly likely. It is more probable that what differential gains there are, occur much lower down in the social scale and derive from the effective exclusion of many Negroes from the labor market. The corporate elite would probably be better off if by some magic they could turn the black population into well-heeled consumers, thereby gaining both bigger markets and social peace. Whether such magic is possible, and why the radicals hold that it is impossible, are issues that we shall come to shortly. In any case it is obvious that it hasn't happened. The war on poverty, which by 1970 had evidently become more of a truce than a war, has never absorbed more than a little over two percent of the resources spent on "real" war and military preparations.[6]

At this point the radical view seems reasonably well vindicated, at least as a description. But is it? There is one rough-and-ready check on rhetorical exaggeration that is almost certain to occur to any literate social scientist, a glance at the latest issue of the *Statistical Abstract* to see if there might be any figures that stood in glaring contradiction to any such judgment. In performing this little test I did come upon statistics that lead me to hold that the notion, rather widespread at least among student radicals, to the effect that the largest single item in American government expenditures goes for destructive purposes, is indeed an error. Since the issue is a very important one with some room for disagreement and great opportunity for confusion, it will be well to pause and discuss it briefly.

The source of the error comes from confusing the proportion

[5] See Edward C. Banfield, *The Unheavenly City* (Boston, 1968), Chap. 4, esp. pp. 73–78.

[6] See U.S. Department of Commerce, Bureau of the Census, *Statistical Abstract of the United States, 1971* (Washington, D.C., 1971), Tables 520 and 378.

spent on military and military related expenditures in the federal budget (which runs to around 47 percent if one adds to national defense expenditures those for veterans and space) with total government expenditures.[7] The latter of course include, along with federal, both state and local government expenditures. When federal, state, and local are treated as a unit, as appears proper when we are discussing government expenditures in general, it appears at first glance that American government authorities spent nearly twice as much on public social welfare as on the military establishment. Here are the relevant figures for 1970:[8]

Military expenses	80.3 billion dollars	8.3% of GNP
Public welfare expenses	143 billion dollars	15.0% of GNP

However, looking at the data under welfare in Table 430, one finds that most of the expenditures come from three items. The first is social insurance under the Social Security Act. Though the explanatory text (p. 267) is not absolutely unambiguous on this point, it is evident that a very heavy proportion of these benefits are paid for out of contributions from workers, employers, and self-employed out of their own earnings. The only reason for including them under government expenditures would thus appear to be that they are similar to taxes. The second item is for veterans programs, clearly the consequence of past wars. The third is for education. Here are the three items and their total:

Social insurance	54,473 million dollars
Veterans programs	8,951 " "
Education	48,823 " "
	112,247 million dollars

What is the appropriate inference? Does the detailed breakdown of the figures under welfare support the case of the radical or his skeptical critic? It seems to me somewhat inappropriate to call these welfare expenses because the term implies a transfer of resources from the more fortunate to the less fortunate. It would

[7] See *Statistical Abstract, 1971*, Figure XXV, p. 372.
[8] *Statistical Abstract, 1971*, Tables 378 and 430.

be better to call them socially necessary expenditures under modern conditions. But the objection is not powerful. The real issue concerns the uses to which a set of resources is put: military versus some more peaceful use. It is obvious that whatever term one uses, these are not destructive expenditures; that their use is indeed peaceful and essentially constructive. On that score it appears that the skeptic has very much the better of the argument.

Any sensible radical would be likely to object that government expenses do not tell the whole story. How about the automobile industry, for example with the deaths (55,000 in 1970), pollution, and destruction of the landscape that it causes? Or how about police and law enforcement agencies and their illegitimate victims? However, unless one is willing to argue that both automobiles and law enforcement should be abolished, and accept and calculate the costs that these measures would involve, it would be necessary to make calculations for the positive contributions of both automobiles and law enforcement agencies. Either way serious answers are not likely to be forthcoming, and the debate becomes hopeless.

Before abandoning this exercise in political arithmetic it will be well to mention the figures on poverty (taken from *Statistical Abstract, 1971*, Table 513). The source indicates that they have been adjusted for changes in the consumer price index:

Year	Number below poverty level (in millions)	Of total white population, percentage below poverty level	Of total Negro and other races, percentage below poverty level
1959	39.5	18.1	56.2
1963	36.4	15.3	51.0
1967	27.8	11.0	37.2
1968	25.4	10.0	33.5
1969	24.3	9.5	31.1

The improvement is hardly attributable to the war on poverty, but rather to trends in the general economy, which had considerable elements of a war boom. The rate for Negroes runs at more than three times that for whites. On the other hand, there is clear evidence of steady improvement here. These data do not confirm the gloomy picture of increasing misery and deterioration that can emerge from reading the daily newspaper—not to mention serious radical discussions.

This little exercise hardly constitutes a blanket refutation of the radical indictment of America's domestic scene. As we have seen, the figures fail us at crucial points. Nor is it clear exactly what a person's moral threshold should be in thousands of victims before we would have a right to consider such an individual morally obtuse for failure to become angry or upset by the number of victims. However, one could reasonably claim that the richer the country, the lower the threshold should be. The exercise is, on the other hand, useful as an attempt to see whether what one believes to be true is actually so. As one who has for some time held that the radical indictment of American society constituted a reasonably accurate description, but who was skeptical about the logic of the explanation, I find it necessary to add several spoonfuls of salt to the description.

The radical position, on the other hand, claims to be much more than a description. By a variety of arguments to be discussed in a moment, they hold that the combination of counter-revolutionary genocide abroad, sops and tokenism along with repression that is more than sporadic at home, constitutes a tightly interlocking and interdependent whole. Though the source of the imperative varies from one radical theorist to another, some emphasizing cultural and to a lesser extent more sociological factors while others stress more purely economic ones, they agree that American society is locked into an historical course headed towards catastrophe, that there is no hope of recovery through the democratic process. Indeed, for a good many of the radicals any attempt to resort to the democratic process seems a dangerous delusion because it helps to conceal the horrible realities of the actual situation and thus diverts energy and attention from the task of bringing about fundamental changes. They see American capitalist democracy as utterly dependent for its basic social metabolism upon the misery that it causes both in the economically backward parts of the world and among the poor in its own population. Further, they perceive *liberal* capitalist democracy as *the* main cause of this misery. Finally, many radicals, especially perhaps the younger ones, perceive inevitable catastrophe as but a way station on the road to a vastly better society. Though the images of the post-catastrophic world vary greatly, from neo-Leninist variants of centralized socialism to decentralized anarchist utopias, they share one common trait. In the new world to come, science and technology, to the extent that they are allowed to continue to exist at all, would presumably be put to work in the service of "the people."[9]

Bad as the present situation is, I disagree with these radical claims for reasons that I hope will become apparent as the discussion proceeds, as well as from considerations advanced earlier in this book. My intention here, and perhaps my delusion, is to construct as accurate an assessment as possible, drawing where appropriate upon radical traditions as well as upon others, and not to engage in polemics.

The most important issues on which I disagree concern the radical rejection of liberal democracy, and more particularly the liberal ideals of tolerance and protection against the arbitrary abuse of authority.[10] Now it is quite true that liberalism in practice has

[9] In passing it is worth noticing that among many non-scholarly (and at times anti-scholarly) radicals "the people" is often a highly elastic concept. It includes everyone who at a given moment is presumably opposed to American imperialism and those who may be expected to join the opposition. Simultaneously, the concept excludes those held to be committed to the other side. Opponents of "the people" run a strong risk of losing the status of human beings. King Norodom Sihanouk of Cambodia, on the other hand, became a member of "the people" as soon as a coup drove him into exile and into the arms of Peking. There is of course much to be said for the notion that cruel oppressors should forfeit their rights as human beings. It would then also apply to those who oppress and kill in the name of "the people." However, given the elasticity of the concept throughout the ages—here one thinks of Athenian and Roman imperialism and its justifications in terms of the Roman and Athenian people—by this criterion perhaps most of the main political and military figures in human history would lose their rights as human beings. If there were some way of enforcing such a principle, it would be worth pursuing this line of thought further.

often been a cloak for oppression. It is a moot point whether that is any more the case now than in earlier times (for example, in England, France, as well as the United States) when liberal ideas were used as legal weapons enforcing freedom of contract, in order to frustrate the demands of factory workers. In any case, radicals do deserve enormous credit for ripping open the cloak of illusions.[11] Nevertheless it is, in my judgment, a very serious and dangerous error to reject the ideal itself, to make a virtue out of refusing to work for it or defend it. (Morality and long-range goals aside, such tactics are also suicidal because they destroy those elements in the current situation that give the radicals some freedom of action.) Such a judgment does depend in part, but only in part, about what one holds to be a desirable future to replace the present.

The one I would propose is a society sufficiently healthy and well informed so that the normal processes of public opinion could take care of dangerous and stupid proposals for public policy. In such a society a Hitler would remain a relatively harmless, ranting curiosity, attracting a few apathetic or mocking listeners on a Sunday afternoon in a park, instead of becoming the master of one of the most powerful nations on earth. Such an ideal society at the present moment hardly looks more attainable than the most extreme anarchist fantasy. On the other hand, from the long historical record of attempts to create a social order somewhat along these lines, a record that goes back to the ancient Greeks and extends up through modern British, Scandinavian, and Swiss history, we have gained considerable rough-and-ready knowledge about the conditions necessary for the existence of such a society. Without pursuing the issue of feasibility any further right now, it is

[10] There are grounds for holding that these ideals have much less to do with capitalism and the rise of the bourgeoisie than has often been supposed. It is at least conceivable, therefore, that in the future the essence of liberalism could survive the demise of capitalism.

[11] Despite disagreement with some of the implications for action, I think that this critical exposure is one of the great merits of Marcuse's essay, "Repressive Tolerance," in Wolff, Moore, and Marcuse, *A Critique of Pure Tolerance*.

enough to assert that any future society that does not preserve and extend the achievements of liberalism, that does not put the ideals into practice more effectively than is the case now, will not be a society worth living in. There is plenty of solid evidence to support such a judgment. The enforcement of orthodoxies has always hurt the masses, not just the professional thinkers. Furthermore, if the enforcement requires real force on any wide scale, it is almost impossible to carry out for any length of time, especially in a world where geographical and cultural isolation have disappeared.

No institutional order can be perfect, and least of all, can it stay or seem perfect to those who must live under it. On that account there is always a need for protection against arbitrary authority, an arbitrariness whose specific content and definition change with changing historical circumstances. Essential to this protection is the possibility of *effective* criticism and complaint. Indeed, this possibility may be the best criterion with which to judge human societies.

There is also, as Conor Cruise O'Brien pointed out some time ago, a huge dose of provincialism and even reverse chauvinism in the claim by some radicals that American imperialism bears the main responsibility for misery and starvation in the economically backward parts of the world. India is perhaps the country where this misery is most intense and where social causes, as opposed to sheer lack of physical resources, are most clearly responsible. Yet, on the basis of at least fairly extensive study of Indian society and history, I can see no significant American contribution to this misery. Nor am I aware of any attempt to argue such a thesis. In the case of China it is very difficult to make more than a slightly stronger case. American influence on the course of Chinese history during the nineteenth century was minimal. Even now, when the United States appears in Chinese official statements as public enemy number one,[12] in assessing the kind and degree of Chinese

[12] Do China's leaders *know* that the USA is a more important enemy than the USSR; is there, even in principle, such a thing as possible knowledge

misery for which American policy *does* bear some causal responsibility one would have to balance off the diversion of China's scarce resources to her military effort against the *élan* and sense of purpose that the existence of America as an enemy provides for many Chinese. It would take a hardy political accountant to cast up such a balance, and it is by no means improbable that the balance would turn out to be favorable for China, even in the rather limited material sense that American hostility enables Chinese society to produce more goods and services with less social friction and injustice than would be the case without the United States as an enemy.

If the argument is couched in terms of Western capitalist imperialism as a whole, it is of course possible to establish closer causal connection with the miseries of the unindustrialized portions of the world. Even in this case, however, the radical tradition, as exemplified in a variety of Marxist and indigenous nationalist writings, contains a powerful element of exaggeration. As I tried to show in my *Social Origins of Dictatorship and Democracy*,[13] which I cite as an excuse for refraining from further discussion, both Chinese and Indian societies contained enormous obstacles to modernization, obstacles very different in each case, with which both are still contending to the present day. Other scholars who have devoted their professional lives to the study of these societies might, I suspect, be inclined to stress this point even more. *A fortiori*, I should think that for Africa the leap into the modern world would have been even more difficult than in India or China, though that is a matter upon which others would have to pass

---

about such matters? (The diplomatic rapprochement between China and the United States that became a prominent part of the news some months after writing this passage and footnote has strengthened rather than weakened their import. Therefore I have let the wording stand in a perhaps anachronistic present tense without claiming any special prescience. Indeed the most important fact about international affairs may be that a very high proportion of any set of factual statements will become true or false if the author waits long enough.)

[13] Boston, 1966; London, 1967.

judgment. That leaves the Middle East and Latin America about which I must also plead ignorance. It does seem to me highly likely that American policy does bear considerable responsibility for the support of corrupt and oppressive oligarchies in these countries, and that in general it has made a serious contribution to the sum total of the world's miseries.

Just how much of this contribution derives from the exploitation of the labor force in the economically backward areas is another matter about which there is enormous room for serious debate. Since there is, as noted earlier, as much obfuscation in avoiding the concept of exploitation as in its rhetorical abuse, the best place to begin an objective analysis might well be American foreign economic relations. On the basis of a sampling of the literature I believe that the issue is still wide open. Because the extraction of oil requires very little labor, there are grounds for skepticism about the applicability of the concept to the Midde East as well as to much of Latin America. Indeed, the opposite charge may be closer to the truth, since very high wages in the imperialist sector of the native economy can distort the wage structure in such a way as to impose one more obstacle to modernization. On the other hand, plantation systems and mining appear to have a rather heavy exploitative component, especially in economically backward areas.

We should also, however, not forget that other factors for which the United States and even the West as a whole bear no responsibility are very significant. Finally, is the implicit radical assumption valid when it holds that these countries could solve their own problems in short order, say in twenty or thirty years, as soon as American influence disappeared? Does not such an assumption fly in the face of all human experience with small states—and for that matter with large ones?

To repeat, these considerations provide no grounds for complacency about the historical and current role of the United States in world affairs. But they do indicate that in crucial aspects radical diagnoses and remedies are very wide of the mark.

If it is not true that capitalist America is the primary cause of the world's current stock of suffering, what should one make of the other main radical claim that American capitalism depends for its very existence on exploiting and perpetrating the misery of the economically backward countries?[14]

Is it true that a counter-revolutionary foreign policy based upon an enormous and terrifying military establishment is essential to the continued existence of "corporate liberalism," to use the radical's pejorative term, that the system would collapse without these props? Do the privileges of educated liberals and opponents of the current drift of American society rest upon the fact that others are willing to do the dirty work for them, such as dropping napalm on Vietnamese children? Is colonial and neo-colonial exploitation the real basis of the affluence that gives liberal critics the economic security and education which permits them to perceive that the "problem" exists in a detached sort of way, but only as a "problem"; not a mortal disease of democratic liberalism? These are anguishing questions. But the answer cannot be based on anguish alone, on an instinctive leap for the most disagreeable answer, any more than a visceral avoidance of such answers or of the question itself.

In working towards an answer, the first point worth noticing is the variety of radical explanations for the supposedly imperative nature of American imperialism. This variety shows that the connection between American economic and social structure and American foreign policy is not generally understood even among radicals, if indeed it exists in anything close to the form they assert. Such a variety also provides a rather strong indication that the thesis of a close and determinate connection may be a considerable exaggeration.

In radical analyses of contemporary America it is possible to discern three primarily economic explanations and one that eschews economics to stress more general cultural and social factors. In roughly advancing order of complexity and generality these explanations and theories locate the source of the imperialist imperative in

[14] A good many radicals of course would also claim that it depends upon corresponding domestic exploitation, especially of the black population. For the sake of simplicity it is better to set this issue aside. For a discussion of the meaning of exploitation see Chapter III.

1) The need for certain crucial raw materials. (Gabriel Kolko)
2) The need for an extra margin of profit through foreign markets and cheap raw materials, a margin that is sufficient to
   make the difference between serious depression and prosperity. (H. Magdoff)
3) The capitalist tendency towards stagnation allegedly due to
   the fact that, under conditions of monopoly, profits pile up
   which cannot find new outlets for profitable investment.
   Under capitalist conditions furthermore the only politically
   acceptable solutions are war (or more precisely the threat of
   war since full-scale war is now too destructive) and waste.
   (Baran, and Baran and Sweezy)
4) Tendencies towards domination and destruction that are
   a necessary and built-in aspect of Western scientific rationality itself. (Herbert Marcuse)[15]

[15] Naturally the very brief summaries given above derive in each case
from my reading of the following books as a whole. Thus the citations that
follow merely call attention to especially important passages. In each case I
have selected a major theme from the author's complex argument. Though
each theme is one the author does stress, it would be a serious error for my
readers to think that this theme was all that the author had to contribute.
Kolko, *Roots*, 50–58, 84–85; Magdoff, *Imperialism*, 177–185, 190–191, 195–
196; Paul A. Baran, *Political Economy of Growth* (New York, 1957), 61,
70–71, 75, 83, 119, 129; Paul A. Baran and Paul M. Sweezy, *Monopoly Capital*
(New York, 1966; London, 1968), 71–72, 75–77. At this point it is worth noting that explanations two and three are quite similar, though the differences
are sufficiently sharp to warrant separate listing. Thus Magdoff, *Imperialism*,
39, specifically rejects the concept of a surplus upon which capitalism
chokes. Specific references to Herbert Marcuse, *One-Dimensional Man*
(Boston, 1964) will be given later in connection with a fuller discussion.
Michael Tanzer, *The Sick Society* (Chicago, 1971) appeared too late for me
to use here, though it is to be recommended as an up-to-date synthesis of
the themes about to be discussed. A large part of Tanzer's analysis draws
upon Baran, Sweezy, and Magdoff, and is subject to the same strictures.
The most original portion is an analysis of the monetary crisis, which I do
not have the competence to evaluate. However, his central conclusion, that
beneath the veneer of international financial cooperation the law of the
jungle still operates (p. 186) appears vindicated by Nixon's famous turn-
about of August 15, 1971. Likewise the adoption of executive controls supports his thesis (p. 222) that the government might try to substitute its

To be convincing, any explanation of American imperialism as a necessary aspect of the American economic and social order has to get around the point that foreign economic activities play a rather small quantitative role in the workings of the economy as a whole. Magdoff faces the problem squarely, and though his figures are slightly out of date, for our purpose it will be best to take his statement of the issue in his own words: "Specifically, how can one claim that economic imperialism plays a *major* role in United States policy if total exports are less than 5 percent of the gross national product, and foreign investment much less than 10 percent of domestic capital investment?"[16] A similar difficulty arises from the official figures that tell us the military establishment has accounted for no more than ten percent of the gross national product since 1955.[17] The explicit and implicit methods that a theorist uses in the effort to surmount either or both of these difficulties go to the heart of their explanations and provide a useful way of comparing and assessing their theories.

As far as I can discern, radical theorists use essentially two types of argument to get around this pair of difficulties. One amounts to the claim that the statistics fail to reveal the actual dimensions of American dependence on its counterrevolutionary foreign policy. The other is to construct a more general theory of American society and foreign policy in such a form that these particular quantitative measurements lose much of their relevance because other considerations replace them. The argument from crucial raw materials is of the first type while that based on the character of modern Western rationality is of the latter. The other two fall in between.

The argument from crucial raw materials holds that the role of raw materials is qualitative rather than quantitative. Neither volume nor price can, it is asserted, measure their significance and consequences. The steel industry, for example, *must* have manga-

---

presence for the invisible hand. How permanent and how effective this substitution will become remains to be seen.

[16] *Imperialism*, 177.

[17] See *Statistical Abstract, 1971*, Table 378 for the actual and estimated federal budget outlays 1940–1971 and percentages of GNP.

nese even though the weight and value of the small amount of manganese, about thirteen pounds for each ton of steel, are tiny. Thus the economies and technologies of advanced industrial nations, especially that of the USA, "are so intricate that the removal of even a small part, as in a watch, can stop the mechanism." Many of these crucial materials, and others used in larger quantities, are either solely available in continents of upheaval and revolution or more cheaply available there. Thus "the ultimate significance of the importation of certain critical raw materials is not their cost to American business but rather the end value of the industries that *must* employ these materials, even in small quantities, or pass out of existence."[18] From this point of view American military and diplomatic policy becomes a perfectly rational strategy. Indeed, Kolko is quite explicit on this point and asserts that the "domino theory" is one "with which Washington accurately perceives the world."[19]

It is worth noting that anyone who rejects this and similar radical explanations puts himself under the obligation of showing that American foreign policy is *not* a rational pursuit of self-interest for the corporate elite. There is then the further obligation of explaining what the policy really amounts to and why it exists.

First, what is one to make of crucial raw materials as the motor behind American foreign policy? After considerable pondering, the argument seems to me rather implausible, at least in this form and with this emphasis. It requires us to believe that somewhere at the back of those who make the basic decisions about foreign policy there is a set of engineers, chemists, and other technical experts who furnish rather esoteric knowledge about the signifi-

[18] Kolko, *Roots*, 53. On the next page he adds, "Intangibly, it is really the political and psychological assurance of total freedom of development of national economic power that is vital to American economic growth." The addition of this psychological dimension may come closer to the truth of the matter. But it weakens the force of the original argument.

[19] Kolko, *Roots*, 85. In my judgment the domino theory is not accurate because conditions differ sufficiently from one part of the world to another to render it invalid. But in this context that is a secondary matter.

cance of manganese and similar matters, knowledge which then passes upward through the bureaucratic machinery to become the key element in strategic decisions of war and peace. Even a moderate acquaintance with the relevant literature on what actually happens in the making of foreign policy, a literature that is by now abundant and revealing, is sufficient to make me find such a conception almost bizarre. If one were talking about oil, that would be a somewhat different matter. But then oil has been turning up in quite different parts of the globe, not only off the shores of Vietnam but also in the North Sea.

The essence of the matter may well be uncertainty itself. Whether it is possible to dispense with a certain raw material or find a substitute is in general something any country finds out only when it has to. It is impossible to know the limits of economic flexibility because it is impossible to forecast where new sources of crucial raw materials will turn up or what kinds of substitutions will be possible, even if it is a reasonable guess that substitutions made under pressure are likely to be more expensive. In an uncertain situation any business firm that needs a crucial raw material is likely to try to assure itself an adequate supply. One device, but only one, is to put pressure on the federal government. If the pressure encounters no obstacles from other considerations (such as spoiling relations with an ally important on other grounds, raising an unwanted domestic howl and the like), the government may well act. Otherwise it would not. Under such conditions the government's policy would certainly display a consistent pattern. On the other hand, this pattern would not demonstrate dependence on these raw materials in the sense that deprivation would have traumatic consequences. As the wealthiest country in the world, the United States has a very large margin within which to maneuver, short of disastrous consequences. It can look for new resources in other parts of the world and use its technological capacities to create substitutes. Ingenuity, substitution, discovery, and where necessary the time-honored custom of trading with the enemy can probably carry the United States a very long way before it faces a crisis. For example, chromite, necessary for hardening steel, and therefore for the military machine that has dropped more bombs on Vietnam than were used in the Second World War, has for some time been coming mainly from the Soviet Union.[20]

One other critical observation is necessary, which is also relevant to the next two forms of radical argument that stress straightforward economic considerations. If an industrial economy has a vital need for certain raw materials within a limited range, it will have similar imperatives whether it has a socialist or capitalist economy. Presumably there could be some savings through the elimination of specifically capitalist forms of waste, although socialism has its own forms. There might also be a considerable savings on armaments, though that is a moot point, since we do not know the extent to which socialism in the U.S. would reduce international tensions. The experience that we have of the spread of socialism to other countries so far is not very promising. Furthermore, whatever is saved through the reduction of armaments might well be eaten up in an increased demand that would result from an upward level-

[20] For chromite the United States depends almost entirely on imports, the main sources of supply being Southern Rhodesia, the USSR, and Turkey a poor third. When UN mandatory sanctions against Rhodesia became economically effective in 1968, the USSR became the main supplier, providing more than half the American imports and Turkey a little under a third in 1969. Evidently the supply was adequate. According to the *New York Times*, November 14, 1971 ("News of the Week," p. 4) there had come to be such a surplus that the General Services Administration had recently proposed that 1.3 million tons—sufficient for a decade of defense needs—be declared surplus. Despite this situation, Congress, out of a combination of log-rolling, negligence by liberal leaders, pique at the UN admission of Communist China, and pressure from American firms with chrome interests in Rhodesia, inserted into a military appropriations bill, subsequently enacted into law, a provision allowing imports from Rhodesia in violation of the sanctions and American treaty obligations thereunder. The whole affair sheds a revealing light on the workings of uncertainty in the context of American politics. For further background information see "Rhodesia and United States Foreign Policy," *Hearings before the Committee on Africa of the Committee on Foreign Affairs, House of Representatives*, Ninety-First Congress, First Session, October 17, 31, November 7 and 19, 1969, p. 205. This source I owe to the efforts of a seminar student, Mr. Michael Doyle, prompted by some observations of Professor Wassily Leontief.

ing of incomes. Thus the net change might not be very impressive, and many basic seeds of "imperialist" conflict would remain. Without going into these considerations further at this point we can perceive that some form of de-industrialization may have to be part of any program, liberal or radical—or a mixture of the two—for altering American society.

The second radical explanation likewise stresses that American capitalism requires for its continued prosperous existence both foreign markets and cheap raw materials. Magdoff's way of getting around the difficulty that foreign trade constitutes a small proportion of the gross national product is both simple and at first glance persuasive. The central point that he makes is that gross national product includes a great deal more than the output of farms, factories, and mines: namely government expenditures, personal and professional services, trade, the activities of banks, real estate firms, and stock brokers. Thus the fact that exports account for only a small percentage of gross national product is deceptive. Considering the output of farms, factories, and mines alone, he estimates that "the size of the foreign market (for domestic and United States owned foreign firms) is equal to approximately two-fifths" of their output. That is certainly a very sizable proportion and there is no need to argue that its loss would indeed be disastrous.[21]

Further examination and reflection, however, reveal that we are a long way from being able to write QED under this variant of the

---

[21] Magdoff, *Imperialism*, 178. On this and the preceding page he also argues that the stake of American foreign business is much larger than the volume of exports, because the volume of capital accumulated abroad has been rising faster than exports. As Richard J. Barber, *The American Corporation* (New York, 1970), 252–256, esp. p. 253, points out, American direct investment abroad, which increased very rapidly after 1955, reveals more about what is actually happening than trade statistics. What it amounts to is the "internationalization" of American corporate giants as they transfer their operations outside the USA, where for a time they have been able to make bigger profits. The critical point, however, is the same as that discussed in connection with trade statistics: "U.S. external investment has been very heavily concentrated in a few geographic areas, most notably in Canada and Western Europe." In other words, the investment has been in other areas of advanced capitalism.

theory of imperialism. In the first place, as is quite widely known. the lion's share of both American foreign trade and American foreign investments is with and in other advanced capitalist states.[22] Therefore one cannot treat the whole of this aspect of the American economy as evidence for the thesis that American capitalist prosperity depends upon the exploitation of the world's proletariat in the economically backward countries.

To be both precise and fair it is necessary to emphasize that Magdoff does not make such a claim. Rather he is talking about imperialism as a whole, and makes no systematic effort to distinguish the exploitation of economic backward countries from the more general phenomenon. It is of course quite common to stress the rivalry among capitalist countries as a significant aspect of imperialism. For Marxists this form of capitalist competition is the main factor behind the two world wars of the twentieth century. But that is scarcely the heart of the radical indictment of America today. To put the argument in these terms greatly complicates the radicals' task, and, I think, very seriously dilutes their claim. For quite some time now the larger capitalist states—England, France, and Germany—have been quite able to take care of themselves. Certainly they are not free of American economic and political pressures. On the other hand, the amount of leverage America can exert is obviously limited. It is also necessary to remember that despite its enormous general power, the amount America can exert at any specific point or in any specific issue of economic bargaining is also quite limited. Even a small capitalist state can therefore have its own way on issues that may be vital for its own social order in the course of diplomatic and economic bargaining.

This observation leads to a more general one. Where does im-

---

[22] For a more detailed criticism of Magdoff see Robert W. Tucker, *The Radical Left and American Foreign Policy* (Baltimore, 1971), 126–132, and especially the criticism of Magdoff's calculations of the return on foreign investment in footnote 41. This book became available as I was in the final stages of revising mine for publication. On some of the economic arguments we evidently reached very similar conclusions completely independently of each other. Note also his treatment of U.S. dependence on crucial raw materials (121–126).

perialism stop and something that it would be appropriate to call normal international trade begin? Is every Volkswagen sold in the United States an example of German imperialism? Is every American sale to a foreign country an aspect of American imperialism, as Magdoff's argument implies?[23] In analyzing international economic transactions we must not forget that the United States *can* produce some commodities more cheaply and of better quality than can other countries and that the United States also imports some commodities because they are cheaper and more abundant in other parts of the world, a cheapness and abundance that derive from geography and other factors as well as American political leverage.[24] To assess the role of this leverage in international economic transactions is admittedly a complex task that cannot be expected to yield precise numerical results. It also seems to me the case that general treatments by "orthodox" Western economists do not give anything like adequate attention to the political setting. Nevertheless it is obvious that *some* form of international trade is an inherent and natural part of any advanced economy, and that if we speak of capitalist, or for that matter of socialist, imperialism we are under obligation to make at least some rough distinction between coercive and non-coercive elements. Without some such distinction one is indeed indulging in pure rhetoric no matter how sober the tone . . . just as the "orthodox" economists' sober presentation amounts to a form of rhetoric on the opposite side of the barricades.

With the thesis of capitalist stagnation as argued by Baran and Sweezy, both separately and in collaboration, we come to a statement that does not discuss the statistical hurdles on the size of in-

[23] See for example, *Imperialism*, 189, particularly the statement about investment-type equipment. In this connection it is worth noticing that while American investments abroad have been increasing rapidly, foreign investments in the United States have increased at the same rate. Between 1950 and 1969 American private investments abroad rose from 19 billion dollars to 110 billion, while foreign private investment in this country during the same period rose from 8.7 billion to 44 billion. See *Statistical Abstract, 1971*, Table 1225.

[24] See Charles P. Kindleberger, *American Business Abroad* (New Haven and London, 1969).

ternational trade and the military establishment. Paul Baran's *Political Economy of Growth*, originally published in 1957, was to my imperfect knowledge the first book to set forth a body of ideas that has remained, even if often at second hand, an important part of the intellectual stock of America's radical critics. It is an attempt to construct a comprehensive theory that relates trends in the advanced countries to those in the economically backward ones. Since I have already criticized some of the main theses about the underdeveloped world in rejecting the view that imperialism bears the main responsibility for their sufferings, the discussion here will be limited to the internal dynamics of American capitalism.

Under advanced capitalism there is, according to Baran and Sweezy, an underlying tendency for profits to rise in the monopolized industrial sector. (Though the term oligopoly seems preferable, that is a quibble.) This tendency leads to the structural difficulty which I think it is both fair and convenient to call that of the unmanageable surplus, though Baran does not use the expression. What it means is that profits tend to pile up in the hands of the big corporations because under present-day conditions they cannot find an outlet in profitable investment. At one point Baran asserts flatly that the big corporations tend to "suffocate" in their own profits.[25] This conclusion rests not upon statistical evidence but upon a series of more general observations. In the first place, monopolies are what he calls privileged sanctuaries, meaning that it is very difficult for one monopoly to entrench on the economic territory of another. (Though Baran wrote before the heyday of conglomerates, it is unlikely that this development would seriously affect his argument.) Secondly, under capitalism the government cannot to any great extent engage in providing goods and services that would render it a competitor of the private sector. Nor can it tax away the surplus and give it to the poor because that would undermine the whole capitalist ethic—for the workers as well as the capitalists. In the third place, the individual firm under capitalism cannot do very much about disposing of the surplus through rais-

[25] *Political Economy of Growth*, 83.

ing wages or other individual acts of munificence because so doing
would cut into profits. Finally, and although Baran has little to say
about this directly, one might add that labor unions cannot be expected to bring about fundamental changes in the institutional order because they have become very much a part of it.[26] Taken
together, these theses add up to the conclusion that under even liberal capitalism there are insuperable institutional obstacles to the
humane and constructive use of America's tremendous technological power. As a result of these obstacles the only politically acceptable way of using the surplus under capitalism is in creating
an enormous military machine and in socially accepted forms of
waste such as a hugely inflated sales effort, gadgetry, and the other
stigmata of what others have called the consumer society.[27]

For those who benefit from the system, war and waste have the
great advantage that they smooth out the worst bumps in the business cycle and do not upset the social applecart by forcing a redistribution of privilege and income. On the other hand, benefits
from the system are sufficiently widespread to make American
capitalism popular: from Oscar Lange, Baran borrows the term
"people's imperialism" to characterize the system as a whole.

In an effort to assess this argument there are, I suggest, three
questions that we should ask. Does the unmanageable surplus
exist? To this question I see reasons for giving an affirmative answer, though I take it that the opinion of non-Marxist economists
would be divided. (One difficulty in judging the argument is that
very few non-Marxists have been sufficiently interested in the issues Baran raises to search out evidence one way or another, even
though among their non-Marxist colleagues both Baran and
Sweezy have the reputation of being good economists.) If it exists,
does it have the political and social consequences that Baran claims?
Is it impossible to eliminate these consequences without a revolu-

[26] The degree to which there is a radical potential among American
workers is of course a hotly debated point among radicals.

[27] In addition, Baran gives some very cogent criticism of consumer sov-
ereignty, pointing out that consumer tastes and wants are the product of
the social order under which they arise. See *Political Economy of Growth*,
26–28. On this issue I have commented in Chap. III.

tionary overthrow of liberal capitalism? To these two questions I shall offer a qualified negative.

As mentioned above, *The Political Economy of Growth* provides no evidence from the balance sheets of individual corporations to show that they had difficulty finding profitable ways to reinvest. In any event such information would probably be kept secret for competitive reasons, or else appear only in highly distorted form. Nor does Baran give any evidence to show that business complaints (and business circles are always complaining about something) would make sense on this interpretation. Instead, the argument is quite general and theoretical. Now the notion that corporations drown in their own profits is not an automatically self-evident one.[28] In this crude formulation it is, I suspect, incorrect.

[28] In the early seventies, when complaints about the cost and difficulty of raising money were rife in business circles, Baran's conception of their central difficulty may seem almost perverse. However, the shortage of funds for investment may be a temporary phenomenon and in itself a consequence of the Vietnam war and military expenses and therefore quite reconcilable with his general theory. The one empirical study I have been able to find, Eli Schwartz and J. Richard Aronson, "The Corporate Sector: A Net Exporter of Funds," *The Southern Economic Journal*, XXXIII, No. 2 (Oct. 1966), 252 asserts ". . . that the corporate sector generates more funds than it can profitably use and dividends are largely a distribution of unusable corporate funds." The absence of profitable investment opportunities the authors see as the main reason for paying out dividends. Though their interpretation of dividends was the subject of challenge and criticism (see *op. cit.*, XXXIV, No. 1 (July, 1967), 150–153), the critics agree that "there is no doubt that the corporate sector is a net exporter of funds." Since the original study covered the years 1924–1964, to a non-economist it looks as though Baran's claim may indeed have a substantial factual basis. However, as Albert O. Hirschman has pointed out to me, there are many reasons for firms to pay out dividends and no special reason for any one sector of the economy to be self-contained. If one wonders why the government does not or cannot tap more of the surplus by taxation, a good part of the answer appears to be the corporations' capacity to shift a very large portion of the corporate income tax onto consumers. On this issue see Robert J. Gordon, "The Incidence of the Corporation Income Tax in U.S. Manufacturing 1925–62," *American Economic Review*, LVII, No. 4 (September, 1967), 731–758, a technical article considerably beyond my degree of literacy in this area. But the gist is plain.

There is also well-known evidence, mentioned by Baran (and of course seized upon by a critical reviewer) which runs counter to any such notion: namely that the share of labor in the national income has remained roughly constant for a very long time, an indication that the capitalist "take" cannot have increased.[29] Marxists too have attacked the notion on other grounds.[30] For all these reasons the basic contention begins to have an air of unreality and, evidently, to require further elaboration and defense. In *Monopoly Capital* by Baran and Sweezy, published in 1966 after Baran's death, the authors include a calculation of the amount of surplus devoted to militarism and waste. Though the calculation tells us something about the allocation or misallocation of resources in contemporary American society, it does not demonstrate that inexorable pressures arise from within the business community for such expenditures, especially since a large portion of these expenses represent resources taken from business by taxation. The authors seem to me to be on much stronger ground in their contention that *without* such expenses American capitalist society would have suffered a depression and crisis comparable to that beginning in 1929 and ended only by the Second World War. By this reasoning the

[29] The size of the capitalist share might of course have remained constant if the share of the big corporations increased and that of smaller firms declined. Baran and Sweezy did not take this line of defense, and I do not know if the possibility has been investigated, though on general grounds it seems rather likely.

[30] I have already drawn attention to the fact that Magdoff rejects the notion that capitalism chokes in its surplus. In general, there seems to be too much of an odor of Keynes in Baran and Sweezy for some Marxists. See in this connection Paul A. Baran and Paul M. Sweezy, "Notes on the Theory of Imperialism," *Monthly Review*, Vol. 17, No. 10 (March, 1966), 15–31, where they analyze the changes in the structure of imperialism that have taken place during the half century since Lenin's major work on the topic. Abandoning as outdated such notions as the export of capital and commodities as the main sources of profit, they stress here the more complex requirements of the big multinational corporations, whose traits they see as the essential feature of contemporary capitalism. With conflicting interests on such issues as tariffs and foreign investments, such corporations do have, they assert, an overriding common interest in opposing revolutions which limit their field of operations and prospects for profit.

unmanageable surplus could *not* be expected to appear in statistics about the operations of specific corporations.[31] It becomes a construct inferred from other evidence and from theory. Though the issue is not closed, I am willing to grant it the status of a scientific reality and pursue the discussion on this basis.

If one grants this point, the unmanageable surplus takes on a new meaning. The Marxists are telling us that advanced capitalism has "solved" the central problem that has faced all historical forms of civilization up until now: how to extract an economic surplus from the underlying population and transmute it into culture and social order. Instead, advanced capitalism faces the historically unprecedented problem: how to use this surplus without making fundamental alterations in the system of privilege and authority inherited from the past and which the productive achievements of capitalism have rendered obsolete. Liberals are disinclined to perceive the issue in this form of historical perspective. Liberal economists will also assert quite vehemently that there are plenty of crying needs and socially useful ways of utilizing America's tremendous productive power. Insofar as they too agree that high military budgets and socially unproductive expenditures have prevented serious depressions, they concede the existence of a surplus. But they deny it is unmanageable. With this liberal conclusion that the problem is *technically* soluble at least some Marxists will agree, but they deny that adequate measures are *politically* possible even under liberal capitalism. That is the real thrust of the Marxist argument.

Why then are they impossible? As the essence of his answer Baran has presented a series of institutional obstacles. Clearly that part of the argument is insufficient. If there were an overwhelm-

[31] On this issue, however, Baran and Sweezy are hardly consistent. On pp. 71–72 of *Monopoly Capital* they assert that ". . . under monopoly capitalism, declining costs imply continuously widening profit margins," and formulate their "law of rising surplus" in the place of Marx's original law of falling profit. To me these sentences imply a realistic conception of the surplus, one that should show up in the statistics. The passage where they hold that it cannot appear in the statistics occurs a few pages later on pp. 75–76. See Paul A. Baran and Paul M. Sweezy, *Monopoly Capital* (New York, 1966; London, 1968).

ing popular demand for slashing the military budget, reform of the economy, and using the resources saved in this manner for improved social services (public health, housing, education, decent public transportation), a Congress and executive would be elected to carry out such a program. Given overwhelming public support and the enormous powers of the government, it is highly unlikely that the business elite could or would hold out for long against such measures.[32] An intelligent Marxist would, I think, acknowledge all this, or something like it, but point out quickly and correctly that for the present any such prospect is nothing but the purest fantasy. To explain why it is a fantasy he would point to the economic, social, and cultural hegemony of the capitalist elite, stressing its fundamental community of interests. That after all is a familiar point in the Marxist tradition. Furthermore, as many intelligent Marxists do point out, modern industrial society with its greater productivity, its ability to satisfy popular wants, and its enormous technical powers of both persuasion and terror (kept in the background for the most part in formally democratic systems) enables the capitalist elite to exercise this hegemony more effectively than has ever been the case before. (On this score the argument approaches the position taken by C. Wright Mills.)

At this point and in this form, in my opinion the most tenable variant of the Marxist tradition, the argument changes its character in a significant fashion. The institutional obstacles inherent in the structure of capitalism, the vested interests of the ruling class and its power, recede in importance. What the Marxists are ultimately

[32] Since many of their administrative skills would be necessary, and a good many of their privileges would remain intact, business opposition might indeed be trivial. There are also reasons to think that a large segment of business leaders would be happier under such a social order since they would really be using their skills in the public interest. One should not cynically underestimate what we can loosely call public spirit. All upper classes profess to act in the public spirit. They are generally successful only so long as by and large their members believe in their job and feel that their privileges do have solid justification. When this confidence wanes, a ruling class is generally finished. This confidence is rapidly waning among the children of the elite. Its loss may be the most significant aspect of the student revolt.

trying to explain, and the point upon which they ultimately rest their case is the *absence of a demand for change*—not the impossibility of change. That, I think, is a crucial shift in the terms of the debate and a matter to investigate carefully.

In the meantime, to sum up the discussion I would suggest that the Marxist tradition has not established liberal-capitalist institutions as the main source of contemporary destructiveness and misery, nor as inherently unchangeable. Nor have the Marxists established socialism as a very effective and promising cure for these plagues.

An awareness that the lack of demand for change may be the key to the miseries imposed upon the world, and in a sense suffered also by American society, constitutes what seems to me the central theme in the fourth set of radical criticisms. For these critics the central fact of our times is a disease of human consciousness. Somewhat unjustly I shall call them romantic revolutionaries and use the term as a label to bring under a single conceptual roof the whole chaotic and feuding mass of radical critics and activists who refuse to accept Marxism as their central guide, much as they accept certain Marxist conclusions, and who are desperately searching for ways to change human society. In fact, a certain mood of desperation may be just about all that they do share. Nearly all of them are students or have recent connections with academic life. Their temper and perceptions change very rapidly in response to external events and their heated internal debates about the meaning of these events. Although these rapid fluctuations have the consequence that any description quickly becomes obsolete, there are, I think, certain concerns among them, and certain general tendencies in their perception of human society, that are likely to be more permanent, and that have in any case existed in recognizably similar forms for a very long time.[33]

[33] Many of their ideas are, to be sure, vague, almost visceral reactions, and at that primarily negative ones. That, however, is the way significant truths about human society often begin. The damage comes later, as the battle over conflicting perceptions begins to be waged with weapons that have nothing to do with perception of the truth, and the right of the stronger determines the outcome.

In addition to the stress on the significance of the lack of popular demand for change, the romantic radical tradition in its contemporary form makes other contributions. One is their rejection of centralized Stalinist forms of tyranny, as well as the forms that the tyranny of the majority has taken in the twentieth century, though there are strong reasons for fearing that, in the unlikely event that they ever gained power, they would both tear each other apart and establish a terrorist regime. There will be more to say on that score presently. Socialism as such they sense is no answer, and on that issue their instincts run in the right direction. They sense further that industrialism itself, in the forms that it has taken so far, is the source of many of the planet's miseries, and that in the advanced countries there is a need for some sort of de-industrialization while the backward ones, they hope, will follow a qualitatively different path. About just what forms the de-industrialization should take and what the future should look like in the United States and the rest of the world, there are almost as many notions as there are individuals who would in some vague sense call themselves radicals. These ideas range from humanized forms of socialism through various brands of neo-anarchism to serious flirtations with odds and ends of oriental religion, and of course drugs.

In other words, there is more mood than analysis among the romantic revolutionaries. If one examines the tradition with our standard questions in mind: "What is the main source of misery and suffering in the modern world and why is radical change necessary to overcome it?", the answers generally resemble theories of American imperialism already discussed, with a few extra touches about the destruction of community by advancing industrialism.

Here and there, however, one does come across serious attempts at causal analysis and efforts to break new ground. Among those whose focus of attention is contemporary America, Herbert Marcuse is quite deservedly the best known. Though he has had considerable impact upon what I have called romantic revolutionaries, Marcuse is also a severe critic of their escapist tendencies and failure to give sufficient attention to political institutions. Here I do not propose to undertake a general analysis of his theories but will limit myself to his critique of technology.

America is the object of Marcuse's criticism merely because it exemplifies to a higher degree than any other part of the world certain tendencies inherent in technologically oriented societies. It is technological man himself that is the central target of his criticism. Nor is technological man a mere abstraction. Marcuse holds to a theory of human nature based on historically modifiable instincts. That part requires no discussion here since most social scientists implicitly or explicitly work with general conceptions of this type; the significant issues arise at a lower level of abstraction. But technological man is a term that stands for concrete human beings with specific psychological tendencies as well as a special way of looking at the world, all molded and permeated by modern technology. The usual view that technology is neutral, that it can be the servant of any social purpose, he proposes to replace with another and very challenging thesis. Instead, the technological project, in the Sartrean sense of project as an end or purpose of organized human activity, contains an inherently and unavoidably destructive component. It is best to put this key point in his own words: "The point which I am trying to make is that science, *by virtue of its own method* and concepts, has projected and promoted a universe in which the domination of nature has remained linked to the domination of man—a link which tends to be fatal to this universe as a whole."[34]

Marcuse of course does not reject technology *toto caelo*. In *Eros and Civilization* he has set out an ingenious argument to show how the destructive component in both human nature and modern technology can be tamed and put to the service of a non-repressive social order. These theories and the Hegelian philosophy in which they are embedded we can set aside for the moment because our task is the evaluation of a straightforward causal analysis of humanity's present plight. This causal analysis is subject, I believe, to the same criteria of logic and factual evidence as any other.[35]

[34] *One-Dimensional Man*, 166. Italics in original.

[35] There is room for honest and serious disagreement here. Many a serious thinker would be likely to maintain that it is illegitimate to separate out the causal analysis from the philosophy within which it is embedded, and that indeed causal analysis is itself the issue that is at stake in the whole

We can begin by agreeing that technology has had very powerfully destructive and oppressive consequences, especially in the twentieth century. I have some inclination to concede the point that these effects outweigh the beneficial ones apparent in modern medical achievements and the conveniences and comforts of modern life, though the issue does strike me as debatable. One can also agree that technology has a certain fascination that imparts a momentum of its own,[36] that scientific analysis often involves breaking its subject matter into its component units for the sake of understanding. But from the standpoint under discussion these are secondary, even trivial, points. The theory claims a great deal more. It asserts not only that there is a destructive component in modern Western science as it has taken shape since the sixteenth century, but that this component is the most significant element in the complicated intellectual enterprise we call science, and that it is the fundamental and most important reason for the essentially oppressive and destructive character of modern Western civilization, including incidentally its "socialist" variant, the Soviet Union.

---

discussion. My reasons for proceeding otherwise and cutting the Gordian knot are these: 1) Hegelian analysis and Marcuse's use thereof, according to my imperfect understanding, accept causal analysis as valid within its own limits. It accepts science but allegedly transcends it. 2) My quarrel is with the transcendence, because I hold that any intellectually valid form of transcendence would thereby simply become a part of science, that is, of established knowledge.

My disagreement with Marcuse's conception of a nonrepressive society is apparent, I trust, from the rest of this book. In capsule form it rests upon 1) a different conception of the role of scarcity; 2) a belief that such a non-repressive social order is incompatible with human societies composed of large populations; and 3) that any future society which does not preserve and extend the historic liberal achievements will be another nightmare. But I agree that the continuation of what has become normal is nightmarish enough.

[36] On the other hand, this fascination, as the historian Charles S. Maier shows, has been compatible with practically every shade on the political spectrum in the twentieth century. See his "Between Taylorism and Technocracy: European ideologies and the vision of industrial productivity in the 1920s," *Journal of Contemporary History*, Vol. 5, No. 2 (April 1970), 27–60.

It is a view that puts an extraordinary load of explanation upon a single factor. How about the impulses towards domination and destruction that were clearly at work in Roman civilization, or even better for present purposes, among the Mongols? Whatever they were, they were clearly very powerful and had nothing to do with modern science. It would not be difficult to think of many similar cases. Against such examples one could adduce some version of an argument in terms of historical specificity; that modern science provides the explanation for *contemporary* forms of domination and destruction. This line of defense requires, however, that one make of modern man and modern civilization something qualitatively different from what has gone before and in a manner that seems to me at least untenable in the light of fairly abundant evidence. That a new cause could appear and old ones disappear in quite this fashion seems highly unlikely. It is clear, for example, that all the main features of modern totalitarianism have appeared in pre-industrial societies.[37] Modern science and technology have greatly intensified and magnified latent tendencies in this direction where they have existed. But it is difficult to regard them as the main cause.

Looking at the issue from another angle, we can ask if there is any alternative to the scientific outlook. The answer depends upon how one conceives of science. If we define it as valid inference from adequate evidence, there is no genuine alternative. In practice science seldom if ever completely lives up to such a definition. Nevertheless that remains the goal. Then the distinction becomes one between correct and incorrect forms of thought, or between science and wishful thinking. The essence of science is the refusal to believe on the basis of hope or ethical conviction. Furthermore, correct knowledge does not necessarily imply the search for control. Actually, control or domination often comes about on the basis of incorrect or inadequate knowledge. As in pure mathematics there is an important aesthetic component in the scientific enterprise, most apparent indeed in the higher reaches of science. Nor

---

[37] For a review of the evidence see my *Political Power and Social Theory* (Cambridge, Mass., 1958; London, 1966), Chap. 2.

does correct knowledge necessarily imply that the destructive component plays a serious role: witness medicine.

Taken together or separately, these considerations, I believe, very seriously reduce the claims of this theory. Perhaps it could stand up better if one distinguished more sharply between science and technology, though the distinction is quite difficult to make. At the same time the traditional viewpoint that science and technology are politically neutral will not do. The results are never politically neutral, but distribute their benefits and injuries unequally through a population, depending upon the circumstances. A crucial element among these circumstances, though certainly not the only one, is the structure of power, authority, and prestige in the society where the scientific advance takes place or that borrows scientific knowledge, as is far more frequently the case, from another country. By and large it appears that a society gets the science and political opposition it deserves, not a very consoling state of affairs.

This state of affairs is distressing only to those who want a more effective opposition. At this point in the discussion the weakness of the demand for change, or its lack of political effect, begins to look like a key aspect of the whole problem of predatory democracy. Certainly it is a puzzling one, about which severe critics of American society disagree sharply among themselves. But before pursuing this clue more directly it is necessary to complete the examination of the radical position by considering two closely related theses on which all varieties of radicalism by and large agree. For them the cold war was primarily a product of the imperatives of contemporary American capitalism. The military establishment from this standpoint has played and still plays a supposedly indispensable role in providing a voracious market for the products of this overproductive economy. Indeed it is rather more in this role as the consumer of an otherwise potentially explosive surplus rather than in its purely military role that the Pentagon presumably serves as the savior of the status quo. Though the first thesis seems to me the weaker of the two, I shall take the disagreeable position once more that although these theses account for a significant portion of the truth, they do not account for enough to be satisfactory.

As indicated earlier, there is a strong case for the view that the onset of the Second World War saved the United States from the very difficult task of finding a way out of the depression that began with the stock-market crash of 1929. But that is a far cry from any claim to the effect that the internal imperatives of American capitalism created the American military machine. Historically it was a rather frantic response to the German and Japanese menace, and a response in which business scarcely played a leading role. Furthermore, German fascism and its Japanese variants were themselves responses to a particular form of capitalist growth. That is one important set of objections to the radical thesis. Another comes from the following set of historical facts. In the years immediately after the war, as the Soviet danger appeared to increase, those policy-makers who favored rearmament to meet the threat, had a heavy task on their hands persuading Congress and public opinion. As Secretary of Defense, James Forrestal was particularly fearful that the rearmament effort might destroy the American economy— "bust the bungs" out of the barrel—an expression he frequently used.[38] Nor was he alone among prominent officials to have these fears. On the other hand, it is clear that Forrestal firmly believed in the necessity and desirability of extending and spreading American business methods or, more bluntly, American capitalist influence, especially in Europe and Japan.[39] Though there are indications of some concern about access to raw materials, I was unable to find any sign of significant pressure for rearmament from business circles in the Forrestal *Diaries* or in the memoir literature by Byrnes, Kennan, or Acheson. Gabriel Kolko, in *The Politics of War: The World and United States Foreign Policy 1943–1945* (New York, 1968; London, 1969), Chaps. 11, 12, and 13, does give convincing evidence of straightforward economic strategy at many points in American policy. However, this capitalist strategy was primarily directed against the British.

In this connection there is some evidence to the effect that *if* business leaders had pursued a strictly self-interested policy in their

[38] See Walter Millis, editor, *The Forrestal Diaries* (New York, 1951), 424–425, 429, 437, 446, 466,. 478, 492, 501, 537. The *Diaries* are quite illuminating on the political cross-pressures of the time.

[39] See, for example, *ibid.*, 247–248, 251–252.

pressures on the government they would *not* have promoted expenditure on armaments. Stanley Lieberson concludes, on the basis of comparing the influence of military and non-military government expenditures on corporate income after taxes for the years 1915–1966 that "a unit change in non-military spending will increase corporate income far more than will an equivalent military expenditure."[40] There is also a third consideration which runs very much counter to neo-Marxist explanations. According to classic balance of power theory, American-Russian rivalry is what one would expect after a victorious coalition. In a sense it is futile to try to discover which side started the process, since both were bound to do so under the circumstances, and independently of their respective social systems and ideologies.[41] Naturally, in the course of this duel both sides sought to preserve and extend their own type of social system and by methods characteristic of and suited to that system. Taken together, these three considerations appear to me to call for rejection of the radical explanation of the cold war.

An examination of the military, to which we may now turn, greatly strengthens the impression that the lack of effective demand for change may be the key to our whole problem. The immediate issue is of course the significance of the military market for American big business. On the basis of a careful and detailed study Stanley Lieberson reached the surprising conclusion that although there is intense dependency on military contracts among *some* very large corporations, "there is no evidence to support the contention that

[40] See his "An Empirical Study of Military-Industrial Linkages," *American Journal of Sociology*, Vol. 76, No. 4 (January 1971), 571.

[41] For a fuller discussion of the whole issue of the cold war see Charles S. Maier, "Revisionism and the Interpretation of Cold War Origins," *Perspectives in American History*, Vol. IV (1970), 313–347. Any future analysis will have to come to terms with the abundant evidence in Joyce and Gabriel Kolko, *The Limits of Power: The World and United States Foreign Policy, 1945–1954* (New York, 1972). This book, in which the authors reject the concept of the cold war as leading one to ask the wrong questions, did not become available until well after the present work had gone to press, unfortunately much too late for the serious consideration it deserves.

the general success of large businesses in the nation depends on substantial expenditures for the military."[42] The essence of the situation, according to this study and evidence presented by the economist Murray Weidenbaum, is the following: In contrast to the situation prevailing as recently as the Second World War, when military orders (which were of course then a very high proportion of the gross national product) affected the whole economy, military technology has become very highly specialized. The consequence has been the growth of a number of huge firms almost entirely dependent on the military market. But, and this is the crucial point, military orders are quite concentrated within this sector, and constitute for the economic giants only a small proportion of their activity.[43]

Two qualifications must be added to this somewhat optimistic appraisal. In the first place, as Stanley Lieberson recognizes, it is very difficult to measure the indirect effects of military expenditures. Pumping large amounts of money into the economy does create consumer and industrial demand. However, as we shall see, it has less of a stimulant effect than other forms of federal expenditure. As we shall also see, the distribution of the benefits is what matters politically, though not in the way ordinarily anticipated. In the second place, there are some indications that the war in Vietnam has slightly reversed the trend towards the specialization of military demand and increased orders for "conventional" items that can be fulfilled by "conventional" business firms such as General Motors, whose share in the military market has long been quite minimal.[44] However, this reversal seems to be temporary, and even the more specialized technology has now begun to run into much sharper Congressional scrutiny and opposition.[45] This opposi-

[42] Lieberson, "An Empirical Study of Military-Industrial Linkages," *American Journal of Sociology*, Vol. 76, No. 4 (January 1971), 581.

[43] Murray Weidenbaum, *The Modern Public Sector* (New York, 1969), 38–39.

[44] See Murray Weidenbaum, *Economic Impact of the Vietnam War* (New York, 1967), 45–50.

[45] By the latter part of 1969 *Business Week* had begun to carry frequent reports of large layoffs in military plants. For the first time since the end

tion can become effective only if widespread popular resistance also develops.

Before going on to this aspect, let us look more closely at the relationship between the military and business. If one takes a list of the 100 largest industrial corporations as published by *Fortune* and sets it alongside the 100 largest military contractors given in the *Congressional Record*, 40 of the largest military contractors will also appear among the biggest industrial corporations. Offhand these figures look like a decisive answer to the question and a strong confirmation of the radical thesis. But they are not. The real issue is: *how important is the military market to the big corporation?* Big corporations can be among the largest providers for the military and *still* be in a situation where military contracts constitute only a small proportion of their total output. The actual situation, it turns out, is one where a few very big firms are indeed almost entirely dependent upon the Pentagon market.[46] On the other hand, for many big military contractors this portion of their sales is very small. Twelve of the fifty largest industrial companies, even though they are among the 100 biggest military contractors, have ratios of military contracts to sales of .04 or less. Within the 50 largest industrial corporations as a whole there are 33 whose ratio of military contracts to sales is .04 or less.[47] These figures hardly support the notion that the loss of the military market would be a mortal wound to corporate enterprise.[48]

---

of the Second World War the military-industrial complex was obviously "hurting"—to use the favorite military phrase so often applied to the Vietcong.

[46] Weidenbaum, *Modern Public Sector*, 39–40, lists ten firms whose government orders exceed half their sales volume. These are AVCO, Collins Radio, General Dynamics Corporation, LTV Inc., Lockheed Corporation, Martin-Marietta, McDonnell Corporation, Newport News Shipbuilding, Northrop, and Raytheon.

[47] All these proportions are from Lieberson, "Military-Industrial Linkages," 568.

[48] There are two possible objections to this conclusion. 1) The military market might be the source of really juicy profits. 2) Even if not the source of especially juicy profits, the military market might be sufficient to make the difference between profit and loss. Given the high level of

Nevertheless, as we have already seen, to think in terms of a mortal wound to the corporate economy may lead us to ask the wrong questions and miss the essence of the problem. The loss of military contracts would have a vital effect on *some* big firms, and

---

fixed capital investment at the top level of the corporate sector, we would expect the break-even point to be rather high, and on this account the additional profits from military sales might be a very vital consideration. Furthermore, in the case of at least some giants the sheer amount is impressive. Thus, according to Lieberson, "Military-Industrial Linkages," 569, although the ratio of military contracts to total sales in the case of General Motors was only 0.31, the contracts amounted to nearly two-thirds of a billion dollars.

In considering the whole issue the first point to keep in mind is that profit itself is a rather elastic concept, because its computation includes estimates about obsolescence and other factors for which it is impossible to obtain unambiguous figures. As Oskar Morgenstern, *On the Accuracy of Economic Observations* (2nd ed., Princeton, 1963; London, 1965), 80, tartly observes: "The idea that 'profits' are an automatic consequence of costs of production and sales on the one hand and receipts from sales on the other is naive and has nothing to do with business reality." Furthermore, according to a study of profits in defense industry by the Comptroller General of the U.S., management records "generally do not provide breakdowns of sales, profits, and related capital for defense work." (See United States, General Accounting Office, Report to the Congress, *Defense Industry Profit Study* B-159896, March 17, 1971, p. 9. Cited hereafter as *Defense Profit Study*.) If management for its own purposes does not make such a distinction (a situation that was the source of much arduous labor and some guesswork for the authors of the *Defense Profit Study* in order to reach its figures), it would appear that the additional profit from defense work cannot be a central consideration in deciding how to get past the break-even point.

Nevertheless, the range of arbitrary decision open to management in deciding upon what is and is not profitable is obviously limited. Hence the data do tell us something, and the direction in which they point runs against both objections. The *Defense Profit Study* excluded General Motors from its calculations on the grounds that its great volume of commercial sales was highly atypical of the big DOD contractors, in itself a revealing fact, asserting that the exclusion would have no effect on the defense profits reported (p. 9). Otherwise it did include the 80 largest DOD contractors (pp. 8, 15). On 74 of these the study gives aggregate data on profits. Profits from DOD and commercial sales are presented according to three different forms of calculation and according to three different classes of firms, de-a damaging effect on numerous others. If so, and more important still, if the corresponding gains from reducing dependence on the military are relatively small and widely distributed, that would be quite enough to explain the very powerful momentum that the military interest has acquired. Once again the discussion takes us back to the importance of any lack of organized and effective opposition. That is very much the situation that Lieberson describes in what is, I think, the most illuminating part of his valuable study. By calculations based on Leontief's input-output analysis Lieberson shows that a 20 percent cut in armament expenditures with a compensating increase in non-military expenditures would create losses in total output and employment ranging from 16 percent in aircraft to 5 percent in electronics equipment. The sector with the greatest potential increase, agricultural services, stood to make a gain of only 2.1 percent.[49] More generally, if some segments of business make large gains at the expense of the public welfare through military contracts, while other interest groups take only minor losses or are able to make some minor gains of their own,

---

pending upon their degree of involvement with defense or commercial operations. Because of the nature of the results we can ignore these distinctions. With one slight exception, all forms of calculation show *higher* profits from *commercial* operations (pp. 19–21). The differences are only slight when profits are measured as percent of total capital investment (TCI) or of equity capital investment (ECI); they are much larger in terms of profit as percent of sales. (See p. 28.) An older study by Weidenbaum, *Modern Public Sector* (1969), pp. 55–58 gives somewhat different results. He concludes that although the defense sector does enjoy higher profitability due to the free provision of working and fixed capital (an issue whose treatment in the *Defense Profit Study* is not clear to this amateur), investors tend to steer clear of it because of the greater volatility of military requirements and hence the fortunes of individual contractors. Since the publication of Weidenbaum's study this volatility has of course become much more apparent.

[49] The figures themselves should not be taken too literally. But if the losses of one group, and that a well organized one, run around eight times the potential gains of another and poorly organized one, it is not very difficult to anticipate the outcome, even if the economy as a whole would not suffer and in fact would probably benefit. See Lieberson, "Military-Industrial Linkages," 571–572.

there will be no material incentive to alter the social order.[50] In
more theological language, for some specific groups the prospective
rewards for political virtue are peanuts while for other groups the
wages of sin are excellent, even if the *overall* social gains from virtue would be greater. Such a situation is not altogether unusual in
human affairs. It is a far cry from predestined fate. But in this
particular situation the consequences that old-fashioned theologians
anticipate only for the wicked, and only in the life to come, can
happen to everybody in real life on earth.

To the extent that the preceding critical review of radical theories of American imperialism is correct, two closely related conclusions emerge. First of all, the lack of any widespread and effective
demand for change appears as the crux of the problem. In the second place, the imperialist imperative does not appear as proven in
the sense that liberal capitalist democracy would necessarily collapse without this feature. The situation is more open, and contains
more possibilities for both good and evil, I would suggest, than is
generally recognized from any point on the political spectrum. By
this observation I do not imply anything remotely resembling a
total dismissal of the radical interpretations. Each factor that the
radicals stress—from the requirements of crucial raw materials
through the cultural effects of domination, repression, and blind-
ness to other social alternatives inherent in the primacy of technology—quite clearly does make a contribution to America as an
important source of the world's miseries. All that I would claim is
that neither singly nor collectively do the radical arguments establish a convincing case for a determinate connection, a presumption
of inevitable and necessary catastrophe—and certainly not of catastrophe as the best device for attaining utopia.

Though the forces that push American society in the direction
of domination and oppression are indeed powerful, they do not
constitute some sort of insuperable imperative built into the very
structure of its social order. The predatory solution to its domestic
social problems is neither a necessary solution, nor the only solution. Rather it is merely the most obvious one, and in the short run

[50] See the suggestive discussion of compensating strategies and their social
prerequisites in Lieberson, "Military-Industrial Linkages," 575–579.

the pleasantest, easiest, and cheapest for a very large number of American citizens.

Nor are the main reasons very difficult to discern. For a very large part of the population the chief costs of the predatory solution fall upon outsiders, mainly now people with dark skins in Asia and Latin America. Such persons are therefore outside the tenuous bonds of identification felt with those who share in Western "advanced" culture. To a lesser and much more indirect extent the costs also fall upon outsiders in American society itself, notably the bottom layers of the population, a large proportion of which also has dark skins, and whose needs are neglected in favor of the investment in destruction. Even many of these, however, make some gains from the predatory solution that are likely to be immediate and tangible, such as temporary escape from the ghetto into the armed forces, while neglect remains merely pervasive. Still others share in the gain even if far from equally. For workers, jobs are preferable to anything that smacks of a dole.

Why should huge segments of the public demand change, as long as others bear the main costs of predatory policies and the mass of the population makes some minor gains from them? Or, one could say, as long as their losses take the form of slow deterioration in the urban environment,[51] increasing inconvenience, or doing without the advantages of civilization that the masses never learned to want very badly—hospitals, schools, housing, clean air. These are issues about which it is impossible to arouse *political* passions, though they are matters about which Americans will make enormous *individual* efforts, once past a certain level of economic achievement. The main preoccupation of most people is likely to remain as usual, with private concerns. Their attitude towards politics, I would suggest, is one of mildly grumbling indifference, with not so latent aggressive tendencies towards any individual or group that threatens daily routines or the limited security of their sources of livelihood. Perhaps many of them

[51] This deterioration Edward C. Banfield tells us is mainly an imaginary consequence of rising middle-class standards. To the extent that more resources are available there are, on the other hand, good reasons for holding that the standards *ought* to change.

would go along very happily and willingly with a better society, one that made a more humane use of its resources and a less destructive one, *if* it became for them as individuals a real and immediate possibility. But they are not likely to do anything about it on their own, or as a collective undertaking. Furthermore, a whole host of experiences and traditions based on these experiences, where they have had to pay the freight for well-meant efforts at improvement, makes very many Americans resistant to and suspicious of "outsiders" who attempt to organize them for any collective undertaking that smacks of overturning the social world to which they have become accustomed.

In such a climate of political indifference, which now shows some signs of passing into history, interest groups can indeed exercise an influence over national policy that is vastly out of proportion not only to their numbers, but is also far beyond what one might anticipate on the more "sophisticated" basis of knowing their place in the social structure. The pluralists may well be correct on certain aspects of the way American politics work. What policy there is comes out of the vigorous impulse of small groups, frequently with limited if dedicated constituencies behind them. The Establishment that America does possess is a rather porous one and relatively open to talent. On the other hand, the openness has been for some time mainly in one direction. It is vastly easier, for the reasons suggested, to promote inhumane and cruel policies than others. Hence the series of vigorous blows by distinct interest groups falls into a pattern. Instead of just Vietnam, we have had of late Vietnam, Cambodia, Laos, Cuba, the Dominican Republic, and others. The pattern is consistent enough to suggest to some observers the illusion of a conspiracy, to others, the illusion of inevitability. What force and consistency there is to predatory policies comes, I think, less from any overwhelmingly powerful structural impetus behind them, than it does from the incoherence, apathy, and disarray of those who would benefit from different policies. Furthermore, as elitist theorists of democracy stress, even when public sentiments *do* take on a coherent shape, as they eventually did in opposition to the war in Vietnam, the constraints on those in authority leave plenty of room for "statesmanlike" acts that flout these sentiments.

It is also necessary to set these domestic considerations in their international aspects. The demand for a decent society—defined negatively as one without war, gross injustice, grinding poverty, persecution for the holding of unorthodox doctrines—cannot be effective in one nation state alone. That would be true even if a substantial majority of the population in all states actually wanted such a society. Since no single state, not even the United States, can possibly exercise sufficient power to control the world for socially desirable purposes, even ones defined in rather minimal negative terms as above, each state under the control of its dominant strata pursues selfish goals under a by no means completely illusory doctrine of national interest. Hence there are strong pressures for social cohesion and patriotism as long as sovereign units continue to exist, pressures that it takes a rather unusual set of circumstances to dissolve.

Thus in preferring a predatory solution the United States is scarcely unique. At the same time no specific predatory solution has ever been permanent. In the American one, as it now exists, it is possible to discern several important sources of instability and potential change—not necessarily for the better.

To begin with the most obvious aspect, the threat of war under present circumstances is a much more satisfactory state of affairs for a predatory democracy than is war itself. That causes casualties. As we all know, a prolonged and inconclusive war with a rising casualty rate, even if it remains but a fraction of the annual toll of automobile deaths, becomes unpopular. In an autocratic country repressive measures can keep this unpopularity under control until the strains of war destroy the routines of daily life to create a revolutionary situation, or defeat, or both at once. Reluctant to use adequate repressive measures, even an imperfect democracy is liable to feel these pressures much sooner and respond to them more rapidly. Should a satisfactory compromise in Southeast Asia remain out of reach, it is not entirely out of the question that there may be increasing pressures for a quick military solution with all available weapons, an event that could turn out to be the "final solution" for all of humanity's problems. Though this eventuality seems improbable, partly because we have lived with it for so long, it is not one to be discounted altogether. Nor is Southeast Asia by any means the only part of the world where the chain of causes that lead to such a result might originate.

There are other more long-term sources of potential change that also derive from war. In the first place, the military solution doesn't work. Vietnam demonstrates the futility of pure technology divorced from realistic political and social analysis. It is perhaps in this sense that the war in Southeast Asia may mark a major turning point in human history. Furthermore, a straightforward counter-revolutionary foreign policy is too expensive in terms of dominant business interests. Though war and an expensive military establishment are not the only causes of inflation and difficulties in the American balance of payments, they are very important ones and widely recognized as such in leading financial circles. And they are by no means the least of the specters haunting twentieth-century American capitalism. As memoirs now make plain, the prospect of controls over prices and over wages (the first thoroughly unpopular with industrial leaders and the second equally so with workers), was a major consideration that led to a change in American policy towards Vietnam and Lyndon B. Johnson's withdrawal as a candidate for re-election.[52] It is one of the nicer historical ironies that his

[52] See Townsend Hoopes, *The Limits of Intervention* (New York, 1969), 179–180, 219, and Clark Clifford, "A Vietnam Reappraisal," *Foreign Affairs*, Vol. 47, No. 9 (July, 1969), 610. The lack of any adequate awareness of these contingencies or serious planning for them is one striking aspect of Hoopes' account, as well as that by Clifford. Even more striking, however, is the absence of any adequate comprehension of the social issues behind the war. In none of the internal debates reported by Hoopes is there any serious discussion of Vietnamese landlord-peasant relationships and their bearing on the war. Societies get not only the kind of science they "deserve" but also the corresponding forms of ignorance, even when the relevant knowledge is (in all probability) abundant and accessible within the government. The *Pentagon Papers*, which became available in the final stages of writing this book, and which I have not been able to study carefully, apparently point towards the same conclusion.

Republican successor found it necessary to try his hand at exactly these levers of control. Finally, as the predatory character of American democracy became more blatantly obvious under liberal auspices and leadership during the 1960s, it generated a revolutionary movement among students, which spread in the form of massive disaffection far beyond the still tiny revolutionary nucleus. By 1970 a very considerable portion of the younger generation of the elite had ceased to accept the legitimacy of the social order under which they were growing up. Nor was the loss of legitimacy confined to convinced radicals. Even if it was mainly confined to the young, the talk of crisis had become commonplace among their elders.[53] Despite all the reservations I have expressed about the evidence and logic in radical arguments, the moral outrage behind them impresses me as thoroughly justified. Vietnam has been enough for that, and there is much more than Vietnam. Whether this outrage and concern can be sustained, whether it will modify American institutions and in what ways, are questions to which only the future will give certain answers.

[53] That the concern was not limited to the academic environment is plain from Albert H. Cantril and Charles W. Roll, Jr., *Hopes and Fears of the American People* (New York, 1971).

VI

Some Prospects for Predatory Democracy

How American society will turn out no one can really tell, though confident predictions are abundant. All that we can be really sure about is that no social order is immortal, that some day this one too will pass into history. Because there is such a thing as creative novelty in human history, I do not think predictions are very feasible in the social sciences, at least not about the most important issues. Nor do I believe that prediction is really the proper task for the social scientist, who misunderstands his own subject matter when he imitates the astronomer. The most that one can do, and a task whose value I do believe to be very considerable, is to present some rough outline of the inherent trends and possibilities in given situations, the probabilities of various types of change, the obstacles to them, and some of the probable costs in human suffering. Imperfect though it certainly is, such knowledge is better than delusion and hope in making political choices, even personal choices for those whose lives will be spent in responding to political trends rather than creating them.

With appropriate allowance for their transformation in a new and changing historical context the traditional terms reactionary, reformist, and revolutionary still serve as the best preliminary markers for staking out the range of inherent possibilities within which individual choice, will, and sheer accident continue to operate. There is also a fourth prospect, chaos and near total collapse, that is generally omitted from such considerations. Here I have in mind the collapse of national authority to the point where human life becomes mainly a war of all against all with tiny islands of law and order under the control of local strong-men waging vendettas against each other. These four categories will do as long as we are careful to avoid treating them as water-tight compartments, and realize that both in the United States and the world at large tendencies in all four directions are at work and influence each other in determining the general outcome.

Because the prospect of chaos has received very little serious consideration it may be well to say something about that one first of all. European society took this form for a long time after the collapse of the Roman Empire. In the twentieth century large parts of China suffered from chaos during the warlord era. Many other examples of near anarchy exist, which is no novelty in human experience. Today it is the essence of relationships among so-called sovereign states. In all sobriety that is the direction in which American society seems to me to be heading, though the prospect itself is quite remote and it is difficult to believe that the trend will not be reversed somehow. With the enormous power that the modern state holds in its hands, its tremendous weapons of both force and persuasion, it does seem perverse to regard chaos as a genuine possibility. On this score modern times do differ qualitatively from pre-industrial times, when, for example, the most powerful sovereign of the age of royal absolutism, France's Sun King, could be characterized by serious historians as the most poorly obeyed of rulers. Yet what could happen if the willingness to use these powerful levers of control evaporates among the rulers, as the willingness to accept their commands and demands declines among the underlying population—if in other words there were a really widespread collapse of legitimacy, a disintegration of accepted codes of behavior, the network of mores and folkways that form the basis of social cohesion? The result would be bloody chaos, not a carnival of brotherly love. It is exactly what could happen if none of the other three prospects, reaction, reform, or revolution gained the upper hand; if all three in their eternal contest managed to neutralize one another. Perhaps the one factor that makes this prospect much less likely than it has been in the past is that the possibility of total extermination now exists. There might very well be a resort to this possibility before the downward spiral of events towards disintegration had run anything approaching its full course.

Today the conceptions reactionary or rightist usually suggest fascism, a term that is used rather too freely. In the United States several of the historical ingredients that have been very important in the development of fascism elsewhere are missing: a powerful agrarian elite that is losing out economically and turns to political levers to save its position, a weak commercial and industrial leadership that throws itself into the arms of the traditional elites for the sake of preserving its economic position, a brief and unsuccessful period of democracy during which pressing social problems find no solution though enough happens to frighten the old elites and make them cast about for conservatism with a mass basis. By now, however, these aspects may not be crucial. Furthermore, adequate substitutes may arise. In a modern democracy, and especially the United States, there is probably much less danger from anything resembling a dramatic seizure of power and much more from what can happen well within the framework of accepted democratic and constitutional practices.

There are many who would assert that the United States already has such a regime. Hence it is necessary to specify more clearly just what a thoroughly reactionary neo-fascist regime might mean: it would force down wages,[1] repress any shadow of racial equality, put actual and suspected dissidents in jail with no "nonsense" about letting them go around the country making speeches while their cases were under appeal, and unleash the military with an end to "half-measures" in coping with America's foreign involvements. We are a long way still from such a situation. That there is considerable popular support for some such program is reasonably clear. Just how much and where it is located in the social structure is a question I am unable to answer.

One crucial element, nevertheless, is easy to discern: the anger of the little man who sees a threat to the small stake he has acquired in the status quo through his own energy and efforts, and who bitterly resents any attack on the institutions, values, and symbols that

[1] In general this prospect means an end to collective bargaining and the destruction of the unions. However, there could also be a substantial amount of de facto collaboration between some unions and business at the expense of the general public, an intensification of trends that already exist.

have rewarded this effort and stand guard over what he has achieved. This reaction to frustrated effort forms a major basis of popular support for reactionary movements wherever they occur: clearly visible among French peasants in their hatred of urban radicals, white collar support for the Nazis. In modern America it is the visceral charge behind conservative trends in the labor movement, especially racist ones. The police riot against bearded radical students is its clearest expression.

Both psychologically and sociologically the decisive element, I suspect, is the connection between frustrated effort and rage. By a series of ingenious experiments psychologists have demonstrated that at least in very many circumstances human beings value what they must work for, *not* that they work for what they value.[2] That connection helps to explain why under different circumstances the little man (and, very often in such instances, the little woman) becomes either a leftist radical who turns angrily against the prevailing social order or a reactionary who hugs the status quo and hates radicals. It all depends on what sort of person appears to be doing the frustrating. In the present American context, for many little men it is the radical, and especially the romantic and cultural radical, who is the apparent source of frustration.

These considerations indicate that lack of demand for change is too weak a term to explain our present state. There is a large reservoir of active opposition. How large and how to deal with it are questions to which I have no firm answers. Frontal attacks and insults by relatively weak groups are liable to exacerbate the situation. Patient rational explanation of who the "real" enemies are and how "the system really works" are, on the other hand, unlikely to get much better results. At a somewhat higher level of abstraction the issue turns into the familiar one of whether radicalism generates counter-revolution. The answer is by no means the pat "yes" of many liberals. What happens depends upon the entire social context. Radical attempts that fail will indeed provoke counter-revolu-

[2] Cf. the literature on cognitive dissonance, associated with Leon Festinger. It is now abundant, and my familiarity with it is limited. The interpretation of its central meaning is mine, and may not be the one this school would stress.

tion and extreme reaction in a society where reactionary forces are already powerful, and especially where the dominant classes can join forces with or utilize the type of popular conservatism just discussed. It is by no means certain that such is the case in the United States today, though the issue would bear careful investigation. In other situations radical actions promote liberal reforms by extracting concessions from the conservatives. To succeed on their own, radicals would have to win at least mass acquiescence in the act of taking power, and have a program that would in its actual workings satisfy major needs of the masses. Thus the issue requires some hard thinking and raising questions to which no very firm answers are possible in advance of the events themselves. Clarification will come, I hope, in the course of discussing reformist and revolutionary possibilities in further detail.

The reactionaries we may now leave with a pair of final observations. Insulting and provoking them to brutal acts (though they often need precious little provocation) *can* be an effective short-run radical tactic when the social order is such that it provokes a wave of sympathy and outrage for the radical victims. That happens when the forces of law and order appear as the ones who violate fundamental American values, when *they* are the ones who appear as bullies. Mere insult, on the other hand, mere attempts to *épater le peuple* for the sake of relieving frustration or conscience, constitute no more than a form of moral self-indulgence. One cannot justify them by the assertion that they are attacks on values, symbols, or institutions that somehow sustain a cruel regime. Pure intentions are no justification whatever for political acts. The consequences for other people are what count in both our action and inaction.

Turning now to reformist possibilities, the first point to get clear is that so far there has been no such thing as a completely peaceful reformist change, at least not in the major modern industrial democracies. At a very minimum, so the saying goes, violence has often served to gain a hearing for moderation. Historically there has been a great deal more to the process than that. By weakening or removing a variety of obstacles, revolutionary violence and civil war, as mentioned earlier, have played their part in creating those democratic institutions that have made subsequent reform possible. Whether some roughly similar process can happen again in the next couple of generations or more is another question. Though the line between revolutionary and non-revolutionary change is somewhat arbitrary, in ordinary usage the word revolution implies a violent destruction of the central government and a violent removal of its personnel. The reformist prospects that we are about to assess by definition stop well short of any such upheaval, though they may include, and have indeed included, in what limited historical experience we have of such change, a substantial amount of what Americans now euphemistically call civil disorder.

The most useful experience on which to draw may be that of England from the late eighteenth century to the early twentieth. During this time there took place three extremely remarkable changes: 1) the transformation from an agrarian to an industrial economy; 2) the acceptance of commercial and industrial capitalists—in still looser language the middle classes—into the political and social order, and the granting to them by the older elites of a considerable share in political rule, most notably in the crisis that ended with the Reform Bill of 1832; 3) later, a corresponding though more limited acceptance of the industrial working classes, through the grant of the franchise, the right to organize, and to strike. Overcelebrated though it may be in some quarters, this combination remains, I still believe, the most significant qualitative change in modern times, perhaps at any stage in human history, that we can reasonably call by and large peaceable,[3] reformist, and democratic. What makes this example particularly fascinating today is the fact that England started out on this course from a relatively repressive base line that has some significant similarities to contemporary America. Partly in response to the French Revolution and the Napoleonic Wars, England had reversed what little

[3] As I have argued in *Social Origins*, the Puritan Revolution in the seventeenth century may have played a considerable role in making possible this gradualist pattern of change. So also, I think, did the dispossession of the peasantry in the enclosures, which I still regard as a form of violence from above. Though these issues have to be kept in mind in any general analysis, they are obviously not the only ones.

movement there had been towards what we now know as Western parliamentary democracy, suspended what little existed in the way of civil liberties—doing this incidentally through legal and parliamentary forms—and became a land ruled by repressive oligarchy. If England had subsequently continued to develop in an authoritarian direction, historians would have had little difficulty in discovering "basic" causes at work during the period roughly 1793–1830. But that was not to be.

Is there anything relevant today to be learned from this experience? Tentatively I shall argue that there is, by trying to see what causes were at work in England, and more important, whether similar ones or possible substitutes might be at work or discovered and encouraged under the very different conditions of advanced capitalist industry in the United States. That such an argument contains a large element of speculation is obvious. Nevertheless it is speculation that is open to checking and correction by others who have more knowledge of the relevant facts.

To begin, it is necessary to specify more clearly the kind of prospective changes for American society that this perspective implies. One might sum them up as a liberalism-with-a-difference, i.e. a liberalism that lives up to its rhetoric instead of using it as a cover for imperialism. To make liberalism a reality is by definition to preserve and extend the historical achievements it does have to its credit and which have been mentioned earlier: civil liberties, protection against arbitrary authority, and a considerable degree of participation in the political process by those whom the process affects. But there is a great deal more. Military expenditures would have to go down by at least two-thirds. In other words, we need not assume a completely peaceful world, but we assume an end to the predominant role of the military machine in the American economy and social order. Along with this change it would be necessary to carry out a wholesale redirection of scientific effort towards humane ends, ends that we will leave negatively defined as not destroying human life or increasing the sum total of human sufferings, miseries, and stupidities. That there would be active and passionate debate over the positive goals is part of the liberal conception. In the economy there would be an end to compulsive and socially wasteful forms of consumption and a very large increase in the services and amenities provided by the public sector. Whatever mixture of private and public ownership and enterprise accomplishes these ends would be the appropriate one. Neither public nor private ownership is an end in itself. Finally, a liberal society to deserve its appellation would have to find ways to end the tragic human wastage—or most of it, because some may well be unavoidable in any society—in the slums and among the rural poor, to give the present domestic victims of American society a decent measure of self-respect and happiness. Though I will readily concede that such a prospect is extraordinarily unlikely, I do not think that it deserves the curt dismissal that unfortunately so often substitutes for serious analysis.

The first and most obvious question to ask is just what segments of American society, if any, might be expected to exert pressures in this general direction? In this connection it is useful to recall that in England the pressures that converged to produce their version of change arose from quite diverse sources. Though capitalists and workers were eventually incorporated into the polity, the pressures came by no means from them alone. Even to speak in such broad terms in describing the outcome is a trifle gross; at any given point in the process the alignment was much more complex. It was relatively small sectors within the various strata that were active, and they were often in loose coalitions with one another across class-lines, for limited and specific purposes. Nor did the eventual outcome exist in anybody's head, except, perhaps in very rough form, in the case of a few professional thinkers. Finally, at the start of the process the idea of democracy as we know it now would have seemed at least as absurd to most thoughtful Englishmen as the program sketched in the preceding paragraph. To most thoughtful people the choice seemed one between a firmly entrenched oligarchy with clear privileges and revolutionary anarchy.

In the contemporary United States *some* aspects of this program would have an appeal to *some* elements among humanist intellectuals both academic and non-academic, natural scientists, educated middle-class women, a section of business leaders, industrial workers, possibly a few farmers and blacks. Such a group would be

very heterogeneous and have numerous conflicting material interests and cultural traditions. For the reasons just indicated which are
based on English experience, that aspect is not necessarily decisive.
Another difficulty or obstacle, may, however, be much more important.

Within this potential clientele I at least find it difficult to discern
any group that is clearly associated with some new and growing
social function comparable to capitalist industry in the nineteenth
century. It is not merely a matter of growing numbers; it is also an
issue of growing confidence in the significance of the social role
one plays, about which it will be necessary to say more in a moment. At a superficial level, youth looks as though it might be
comparable. (Here we are obviously not talking about its still tiny
segment that has been quite thoroughly radicalized, and for whom
any such prospect as that outlined would be anathema.) Youth
appears to be growing as a section of the total population, though
demographic projections have a way of requiring reversal rather
frequently, and youth is certainly gaining an increasing amount of
political attention. On the other hand, it is difficult to perceive any
new social function that youth as such does or can perform that is
likely to gain recognition from the social order as a whole. If anything, the reverse seems to be in the cards, and should society survive and be grateful some day, it will be because young people
helped to *stop* certain functions from going on. There is also the
obvious fact that young people do not stay young indefinitely,
even if their place is taken by others.

In emphasizing the difficulties there is nevertheless a strong risk
of succumbing to the disease known as the myopia of present-
mindedness. It is not altogether possible to rule out the prospect
that in a program of liberalism-with-a-difference there could be
sufficient attraction for enough people to mount an effective challenge to the status quo. The incentive, be it noted, need not be
completely material, even if that helps tremendously. A great deal
of the reward can come from the effective performance of a task
about which the individual has strong moral convictions concern-
ing its social importance.

That these moral convictions would have to change considerably from prevailing ones is obvious. There are at the same time some good reasons for suspecting that they might have to change in a way that is not generally anticipated. Here are another severe obstacle and set of considerations that apply, be it noted, with even greater force to some radical visions of the future.

The general drift of modern society, it seems reasonably plain, is to require less hard work. This tendency is welcome to all those even slightly to the left of center and beyond. Likewise, in advanced circles the view has become fairly widespread that America is if anything overdeveloped economically, that not only the direction of the economy should change but also the general level and amount of economic activity. What does this mean in concrete human terms? All along the line it means slimmer economic pickings, and less room for the energetic innovator. One highly likely consequence is that those who already do have special skills and occupations would seek to protect them more strongly. The end result of a generally static economy could well be a return to a guild-like structure, even with overtones of caste.[4] That such a situation with a rapidly growing population would lead to a purely destructive explosion seems highly probable, indeed almost inevitable. With a static population the arrangement might just possibly work. Indeed, it may in the not so long run be almost the only way human society can survive. But the costs of this prospect, or something like it, will have to be taken into account. Conceivably, service occupations, which are now an area of expansion, can take up a great deal of the slack. Nevertheless a saturation point exists, especially if one keeps in mind that many present service functions are connected with areas of the economy devoted to the type of compulsive consumption that has been postulated as due for a decline.[5]

---

[4] It would also greatly intensify a problem that already looks insoluble, bringing "unemployables" into an orderly society and giving them a decent measure of self-respect.

[5] Perhaps I am being too pessimistic in ruling out as a social and psychological impossibility a society in which the mass of the population devotes no more than a tiny fraction of its time to "socially necessary" and "useful" work. Nevertheless I do doubt that the mass of human beings are

The considerations just mentioned have already led the discussion towards the kind of opposition to be expected. That liberalism-with-a-difference would encounter enormous vested interests with substantial popular support is quite obvious. Again, however, that was true in England. Two general conditions appear to be necessary in making a relatively peaceable transition possible. One is that a substantial section of the elite has material room for maneuver. It must be able to make concessions when other elements in society press for them, a pressure that includes the threat of violence and occasional resort to it. There are reasonably sensible grounds for holding that such is the case in contemporary America, especially in the most powerful business circles. On this score it is possible to form the impression, from reading a variety of business publications and other sources, that those in the seats of economic power are actively looking for just what concessions to make. The matter would bear looking into, but we may leave it at that.

The other condition is more complex. The essence may be that for a peaceable and democratic transition elites must invent or adopt new ways of satisfying the "felt needs" of the society (which elites do a great deal to create and sustain). A substantial section of the elite must be able to shift to the new task and perform it satisfactorily. A demand, on the other hand, for the *elimination* of a particular social function and by implication the persons who perform it, make such a change impossible. The savagery of the Catholic Church towards medieval and later heresies arose from the fact that heretics generally asserted that it was possible for ordinary human beings to achieve a direct contact with God. On the surface a harmless idea, it nevertheless challenged the necessity for the priestly hierarchy, its entire *raison d'être*.

It is possible that this pair of conditions, room for material concessions on the part of the elite and the possibility for changing its social basis and function in a less repressive direction, may be the most important factors of all that influence the prospects of liberal

---

capable of just enjoying themselves most of the time, at any rate in a way that makes them tolerable to each other. At least the illusion of a wider and deeper purpose seems necessary. What illusion might serve?

changes that go beyond very limited patchwork decorated by complacent rhetoric. To avoid misapprehension it is necessary to emphasize that these conditions do not apply to the whole of the dominant strata. Again if English experience is any guide, only a small and crucially placed segment is sufficient. Colonel Blimps and their counterparts are likely to be a majority in any dominant stratum that has been in power for more than a generation and don't really matter very much.[6]

With these qualifications and clarifications, how does the situation look in the United States? There are several very severe obstacles that would have to be overcome, though they do not seem to me adequately characterized by the traditional conceptions of private property and the profit motive. One has already been mentioned, the necessity for a quite considerable lowering in the overall production and distribution of material goods (though *not* of services, whose character would have to change) and the consequent reduction in economic opportunities. Furthermore, many forms of activity would have to come to a stop, as within the military and wasteful forms of production and consumption, to which there would be enormous resistance. Other economic activities would have to take place in a way that sharply reduced their costs to the general public and increased the costs to their immediate proprietors. Industrial pollution is an obvious example. Finally, there would have to be a substantial narrowing of income and prestige differentials, though nowhere near complete equality.

What these considerations add up to is an overall reduction of the general importance of economic life in American society as well as a very great change in the way economic tasks are performed. That would only be possible within a generally reformist and democratic framework, provided other forms of activity took up the slack. They would also have to take up the slack in a manner that provided a challenge and a considerable degree of excitement. There would still be a need for administrative skills of a

---

[6] That there is the possibility of radicals making huge miscalculations about the significance of this limited segment is obvious. Ferdinand Lassalle's behavior in relation to Bismarck looks like an example of such miscalculation.

high order, indeed a higher order than exist now, since the situation would require not only tact in dealing with refractory human beings but a broad and accurate vision of the world. There would have to be prestige for the leaders in these new activities and a general willingness to devote resources to them.

It is not easy to discern just what these new activities might be. The traditional ones, an increase in public services such as health, education, public transportation, housing—and a drastic change in their quality—are matters about which it is very hard to arouse wide popular enthusiasm. Again, however, that may be a case of the myopia of present-mindedness. Indeed to call them public services, to draw a distinction between the public and private sector—as Murray Weidenbaum has pointed out from a perspective very different from that taken in this book—may be to darken counsel and obscure the central issues. Does it really matter that the postal service is a public corporation and the telephone service is a private one when both are deteriorating and increasingly expensive? Would a talented executive really prefer to do a stupid job at high pay or an intelligent job at substantially less pay? And how exactly does one determine that the intelligent jobs do get done properly: those that diminish human suffering and contribute to the comforts and amenities of our short span on this planet, that also give a meaning and purpose beyond this pitifully short span? To such questions there are, I suspect, reasonably definite negative answers and no final or transhistorical positive answers.

It is obvious that any such shift in the basis and character of the elite carries with it the danger that the whole process may become nothing more than an operation in public-relations flummery. There is already enough talk about the social responsibility of big business to raise quite justifiable suspicions along precisely these lines. It is highly unlikely that the change could take place successfully without vigorous pressure from other sectors of society. Through relentless critical exposure radicals might play a very important role, no matter what their intentions. Purely negative threats, however, would be quite insufficient.

Mention of the radicals brings us back to the part that violence

might play in bringing about an essentially reformist and democratic transition. That, however, is embedded in a much larger
set of issues. In order for the transformation to succeed within a
predominantly peaceful framework, there has to be some degree of
shared values and goals among the political contestants. More specifically an influential segment of the elite would have to recognize
elements of legitimacy in the demand for changes. Correspondingly, those who sought change would have to believe that the
dominant groups were not wholly and totally discredited. On both
sides there would have to be a powerful moral reluctance to resort
to force. But on the side of the dominant groups there would have
to be a willingness to use it in the face of genuine insurrectionary
dangers, along with a calmness and freedom from panic in judging
the degree of such danger. It is necessary to recall that part of the
reason for what successes gradualism has enjoyed is the willingness
to use enough force to demonstrate that violence is an unsuccessful
and dangerous tactic. Those seeking changes, on the other hand,
would have to create the illusion that there was a powerful and
unified popular demand for the changes, or more accurately for
certain decisive yet limited aspects of these changes (such a unified
popular demand is probably *always* an illusion), and that failure to
make key concessions implies enormous if somewhat vague dangers.[7]

On balance it looks now as though these observations describe reasonably accurately what is not taking place. Current talk at the end
of the 1960s and early 1970s at any rate, was mainly about polarization of opinions, the loss of faith in American institutions by
the young and the blacks, etc., etc., a process deplored by some
and welcomed by others. I do not think that the evidence is that
clear or that the process is necessarily irreversible, at least not yet.
Even among the young there remains an enormous reserve of confidence in the possibilities of quite far-reaching social changes
within a liberal framework. It certainly exists among those over the
magic dividing line of thirty. Radicals too, I suspect, often share

[7] These observations are based on my interpretation of Joseph Ham-
burger, *James Mill and the Art of Revolution* (New Haven and London,
1963).

this belief in latent form because of the efforts they make to avoid displaying it and appearing naive before their more militant comrades. We also have to remember that recurring crises mobilize moderates as well as radicals. Quite frequently in fact the radicals find themselves swamped by the wave of moderation following a crisis that they have tried to provoke or from which they have tried to profit. In sum the situation is probably still fluid enough for gifted leadership to make a large difference.

Beneath this confusing ebb and flow of opinion, one may nevertheless, discern something more solid. If liberalism-with-a-difference, or perhaps better a somewhat radicalized liberalism, fails to achieve at least some concrete and striking success on the national level fairly soon, the polarization will probably intensify with disastrous results. More and more people will not want "reform," they will want something totally different. Without some concrete success this version of a belief in the democratic process cannot sustain itself. At the present writing a serious clipping of the military wings would be such a success; a few years hence it might be something quite different. To define the success more closely in advance would be fruitless. It will be easy enough to recognize if it ever happens.

So far the discussion of the prospects of peaceful transformation has considered the United States as an isolated social unit, a necessity for orderly exposition but a crude violation of reality. There is at least one more necessary condition that historical experience suggests: the absence of a serious foreign threat. Serious in this case one can define somewhat more closely as meaning that no influential segment of the society feels convinced over a prolonged period of time that the national existence and way of life face a dangerous threat from outside its borders. That the garrison state is incompatible with *any* version of a liberal social order seems so obvious as to be scarcely worth mentioning. A liberal society is also in all likelihood incompatible with the active military pursuit of world hegemony or its rigid defense. It is not, on the other hand, as English experience in the Second World War indicates, necessarily incompatible with some periods of strenuous military effort.

Do these observations imply that the United States would have to sink to the level of a Sweden or a Switzerland before liberalism-with-a-difference became possible—in which case the prospect is indeed totally unrealistic? Possibly that is so, although I suspect that the thesis is unrealistic for a different reason: namely that the peaceably liberal characteristics of these societies have been dependent upon the violence of others, including the United States. In any case there are more immediately relevant issues that have to be raised. Would such a liberalism as that envisaged here be dependent upon continued exploitation of the backward world? Was not English liberalism itself so dependent during the industrial revolution and the nineteenth century? Is not the whole model therefore misleading? Does not the causation work the other way around from that just asserted: may not liberal society in *any* form depend upon world hegemony and continued exploitation, and is not that exactly what the English example demonstrates?

As is the case with every issue raised in this book, there is enough in these questions to keep many scholars busy for their whole lifetime. Many *have* devoted their lives to important aspects of them. Since we have already been over the issue of American dependence on this form of exploitation, I will confine myself to some very general observations. The danger that such exploitation would continue is of course a real one. There is also the moral issue of how much of a right Americans have to make other people suffer in order to solve their own problems peaceably—as well as the counter-question of whether a revolutionary solution may not make everyone suffer a great deal more. On the other hand, there are reasons for holding that the connection between liberalism and foreign exploitation, though it certainly has existed, is not a necessary one at all in the first place. Indeed, if it were necessary, nineteenth-century England would be the classic example rather than contemporary America. There are plenty of facts lying around that can be pulled together to construct the portrait of nineteenth-century English liberalism as the grinning hypocrite sitting upon the backs of those who in turn wielded the lash over plantation slaves and created the discipline of the machine. The portrait is by no means altogether false. But there are some good reasons for being skeptical about whether it captures the essential truth, the real relationships among the various factors, because it rests on a very dubious assumption. It is a viewpoint that reduces all trade to coercive cheating and ignores the increased capacity to satisfy human wants that comes about through the machine.[8]

If there are good grounds, then, for holding that a liberal society with plenty of radical fire under it need not depend for its existence on foreign exploitation, how about the other side of the coin, the foreign revolutionary threat? I have never believed that communism was no threat at all or that the communist threat was mainly the figment of a fevered and manipulated American imagination. On the other hand, there are quite a few indications that as communism spreads it becomes less of a threat. It seems to be less of a threat both in moral terms, as a threat to liberal values, and in the strictly amoral terms of strategic planners. The most important reason for this somewhat ironic development is that as the revolutionary movement has spread, it has had to cope with the specific peculiarities of new countries and acquired many of their older rivalries along with its own form of internal disputes. The more successful the revolutionary movement becomes, the more its component parts differ and quarrel with each other. For that matter when the movement was unified in the Stalinist era, the danger did not deserve to be called revolutionary. In the absence of either a powerful strategic threat or a serious revolutionary one, the United States could and probably would return to the usual behavior of allying with some revolutionary regimes, betraying others, quarreling and fighting with still others, all rather independently of their specific coloration on the political spectrum. To be sure, if a single revolutionary wave suddenly deprived the United States of *all* foreign economic contacts, this country would be, to say the least, in a highly awkward spot. But such a prospect, I would suggest, exists mainly in the minds of a few quite unduly optimistic radicals and some unduly pessimistic Pentagon planners. Unless one believes that capitalists can trade only with capitalists

[8] Cf. the Marxist notion that machines cannot create value, that the machine merely imparts the value stored up in it in the form of "dead labor," i.e. the human labor required to make the machine.

and can even then trade successfully only where they exercise political hegemony, there is no overwhelming reason for the United States even now to become very concerned about what happens in these countries.

These comments on international affairs may be far too optimistic. Real threats can arise in ways that are very hard to anticipate, as when a political genius exploits an ambiguous situation to create a powerful expansionist state out of highly unpromising materials. The Chinese, the Russians, and the Americans cannot be expected to accept anybody's definition of reasonable international behavior except their own, even with enormous changes in their respective social systems. There is no particular reason to think that these trends will make them move closer to agreement rather than further apart. Nevertheless neither the present juncture in international affairs nor what appears to have been the underlying drift of the past twenty years present, as far as I am able to discern, insuperable obstacles to the kind of domestic transformation just discussed. America is certainly powerful enough and rich enough to afford a great deal of social experimentation if that is what the mass of the people want. But will it happen?

Hopefully abusing the scholar's right of lapsing into incorrect prophecies in a speculative essay, I will say flatly that I do not think that the general prospect of liberalism-with-a-difference is in the cards that history will deal the United States. No obstacle is necessarily insuperable, but all are formidable. The most serious one, if the preceding analysis is near the mark, is discovering and rewarding a whole new series of socially useful activities, as getting and spending (and there are lots of those who have not yet got enough to spend) necessarily recede into the background and change their form along the lines hinted at. The potential constituency is too weak and divided, the necessary sacrifices too great. Then there is indeed the international arena of dog-eat-dog that can always provide a genuine or false pretext for avoiding domestic issues.

Still, odder things have happened in human history. The desire for such a society is firmly rooted in Western traditions that go back as far as the Greeks. We cannot really be sure, which is one good reason for discussing the issue at all. And another reason is that all the other prospects look even worse in terms of the human suffering they are liable to produce. That is certainly true of the reactionary prospect and of sheer chaos. Under existing conditions it is also true, I believe for reasons about to be set out, of the revolutionary prospect.

On that score the first question to ask may be: how seriously should we take the question itself? Is revolution in America a prospect that deserves serious consideration? For that matter, does *anyone* know what a revolutionary situation is or a potentially revolutionary one, and equally important, what is *not* a revolutionary situation? There are evidently all sorts of shadings and gradations here, among which even an expert may go astray. Two years before the Russian Revolution Lenin remarked that although the socialist revolution was sure to come, his generation would not live to see it. To give away the answer before telling the story, in a manner opposite to that of the old-fashioned detective story, I will assert two propositions. The first is that the United States is not now in a revolutionary situation, though it could conceivably arrive at that stage if certain conditions, to be specified in due course, are met. The second proposition is that even if the conditions are met and a large-scale attempt at insurrection does occur, it is unlikely to turn out the way any of its current proponents hope.

These propositions I do not intend or expect to prove in any rigorous sense of the term. Such attempts at pseudo-scientific prophecy I am quite content to leave to convinced and genuine revolutionaries. That sort of faith may be necessary to move the world. Since such certainty about the future inevitably lacks a solid foundation in evidence and logic, the scholar must dispense with it. In letting others move the world the scholar has no reason to look at them wistfully. The men of action and conviction have failed enough of late to warrant reversing a famous apothegm of Marx: philosophers have tried to change the world; now it is time to try to understand it.

For that matter everyone interested in the problem, whether activist or observer, suffers from the same limitation: all they have to go on is past experience. Revolutionaries themselves, like generals and scholars, march into the future facing resolutely backward. Puritan revolutionaries looked back into the Bible; the French to the Romans and the Greeks, the Russians to the French and to what Marx thought he saw of the future in looking at nineteenth-century capitalism, an imaginary world that was about as far from Russian conditions as could be imagined; latest of all comers, the Chinese communists looked back to the Russians and again to Marx while they went ahead and did something that had very little to do with either of them. To the extent that revolutionaries did succeed, they often did so in large measure by avoiding slavish adherence to past models and by displaying ingenuity in devising new social mechanisms and new policies for unprecedented situations. The scholar has no completely effective way of coping with this element of genuine historical novelty. All the scholar can do is examine the variety of conditions that have led to the creation of revolutionary situations and movements in the past, and that have affected the subsequent fate of these movements. Then one can try to determine the extent to which such conditions may or may not apply, currently or in the foreseeable future, to the situation in the United States. Significant though the element of creative improvisation may be in politics, it never starts from scratch, and it always works within a set of limiting conditions.[9] With some imaginative insight, and perhaps more luck, the scholar may also perceive what improvisations the revolutionaries are likely to attempt, and assess their probable consequences with the help of knowledge about these confining conditions. In all these ways historical reflection, even if it cannot guarantee certainty, can be very helpful in distinguishing between rhetorical pipe dreams and genuine possibilities.

As we turn to the historical record for whatever light it may cast, the first point worth noticing is that revolution itself is a quite recent historical novelty. Here of course it is necessary to be clear about what we mean by revolution. Angry uprisings by

[9] For a brilliant discussion of the limiting conditions on past revolutionary movements see Otto Kirchheimer, "Confining Conditions and Revolutionary Breakthroughs," *American Political Science Review*, Vol. LIX, No. 4 (December, 1965), 964–974.

segments of the lower classes stretch back at least as far as the slave revolts of antiquity, though there are striking differences in the extent to which the different branches of human civilization have been subject to them. These revolts, on the other hand, either lacked altogether or displayed to a very minimal degree one element crucial to modern revolutions, the idea of somehow using the anger of the lower classes not only to destroy the prevailing social order, but also to create a new and different one in which the traditional forms of oppression would cease to exist. As late as the Revolt of the Netherlands in the sixteenth century there was, as far as I have been able to ascertain, no conscious and deliberate attempt along these lines, and no more than preliminary beginnings in England's Puritan Revolution during the next century. The programmatic use of revolutionary violence did not appear for another century, when it came to full bloom in the French Revolution.

The inferences one can draw from the fact of historical novelty are in this case faintly hopeful. Though revolution has been an important social invention in mankind's record of attempts to cope with the miseries he has made for himself, not even the most dedicated revolutionary can claim that it has been an unmixed blessing. In fact of course it is an enormously cruel and wasteful way of solving human problems, one where so far at any rate the main burden of suffering has fallen upon masses of little people. Since revolution is, unlike war, a relatively recent social invention, there is at least some reason to anticipate that it may constitute no more than a temporary phase in social evolution and that man may be able to perfect less cruel and violent methods of social adaptation. Just how much time human beings may have for social discovery before they destroy one another or make life unbearable in some other fashion, remains of course uncertain.

In previous patterns of revolutionary change it is possible to discern three sets of mutations that have occurred within the dominant classes prior to the outbreak of serious revolutionary violence. One of these Crane Brinton has named "the desertion of the intellectuals." It is something much deeper than a desertion: a challenge to the prevailing modes of thought and to the whole perception of the possible causes and remedies for human suffer-

erals' war," rapidly intensified and spread this rejection. All that is familiar and requires no elaboration. So far the decay has mainly been confined to young people and to blacks, and in all likelihood a minority even among both of these. By itself, however, size is not decisive. Societies do not come apart by majority vote. The intensity of disbelief, willingness to act, and the location of disbelievers in the social structure are more important. On this score it is reasonably plain that a very significant element among those "normally" expected to run American society within the next ten years now bitterly reject it. The same is true, though for very different reasons, of an equally significant element of those "normally" expected to remain patiently and uncomplainingly at the bottom of the heap. The bitterness is sufficiently severe and located in sufficiently strategic parts of the social structure for me to hazard the estimate that at least one pre-condition for revolutionary change may well have been fulfilled. But the loss of legitimacy is only one pre-condition, and by itself quite insufficient for revolution.

By itself, that is, without the rise of corresponding ideas about how society can and should be organized, the loss of legitimacy leads only towards chaos. So far no intellectual scheme has emerged as a clear alternative, certainly not in the sense that Enlightenment doctrines, for all their variety, came to constitute an alternative to traditional views of the social hierarchy. For reasons mentioned earlier any such view will probably have to take account of the existence of a very considerable industrial plant and of continuing sovereign states. Though a certain amount of de-industrialization may be both feasible and highly desirable, a real back-to-nature movement would be the equivalent of dropping a hydrogen bomb. Nor are there serious grounds to anticipate a worldwide revolution ending in the brotherhood of man. For the American system simply to fall apart through the failure of the belief system, those who command the political and economic levers would have to be quite unable to recruit any successors. So far that situation seems a long way off. All sorts of presently unpredictable trends could emerge in the meantime, including intellectual movements to restore and revitalize the existing order, a twentieth-century version of counter-reformation. Even if restoration movements never really succeed in restoring the old order, they can slow up changes and steal the lightning of their competitors by adopting parts of their program.

It has been necessary to go into this aspect at some length because for some time there has been much talk to the effect that a cultural mutation is taking place, and that by itself this cultural mutation under the conditions of modern industrial society may render the classical forms of revolution obsolete. The argument is a serious one for which only the future may provide a serious assessment. (Naturally, if it *does not* happen that way, that would not prove that it *could not* happen that way. Only if the cultural mutation succeeds in a manner approximating the hopes of its promoters will there be proof.) Though I agree that a cultural mutation of sorts may be under way, and indeed that it may have quite significant consequences, I do not think that this change in the realm of thought alone can carry the political freight that its optimistic advocates hope will be possible. As a new locomotive of history under changed circumstances it just won't do.

A second mutation preceding past revolutions has been the appearance of very sharp conflicts of interest within the dominant classes themselves. In all major revolutions so far the symptom has been apparently insoluble financial problems. Behind the symptom have been acute disagreements—insoluble contradictions might for once do as a meaningful empirical term here—about how to resolve stresses posed by the rise of new social relationships and, more specifically, about which social groups are to bear the costs of these new arrangements. This split in the dominant classes has quite different causes in successive historical epochs and in different countries. Hence there is little to be gained by efforts to reduce it to a single pattern of events. Whether one will occur in the United States depends upon how long and how satisfactorily the predatory solution of token reform at home and counter-revolutionary imperialism abroad continues to work. If the arguments presented earlier are correct, the American system still has considerable flexibility and room for maneuver including strategic retreat. There is even a slim chance of peaceful change within the democratic framework, or rather of recreating this framework with and through a limited amount of disorder that falls short of real revolutionary upheaval. Indeed it is worth noticing that up to this point in the analysis the generalizations apply, with only slight modifications, to non-revolutionary changes.

They cease to apply when we come to the third mutation among the dominant classes—loss of unified control over the instruments of violence: the army and the police. Where a section of the dominant classes breaks off and takes with it part of the armed forces, historians are accustomed to calling the result a civil war. When the police and the armed forces refuse to obey, they are likely to call it a revolution. Actually, as in the Chinese Revolution, there can be a mixture of the two processes. In the case of the United States as early as 1970 there began to be a number of public clues to the effect that decomposition had set in among the military forces. As in earlier cases the process began among garrison troops. One indication has been the well publicized investigation of racial clashes among troops stationed in Germany. Another, especially vivid one, which recalls the behavior of Russian troops prior to the collapse of 1917, appeared in the form of a letter from a soldier in Vietnam, published in the *New York Times*, November 21, 1970:

> "They have set up separate companies for men who have refused to go out to the field. It is no big thing here anymore to refuse to go. If a man is ordered to go such and such place he no longer goes through the hassle of refusing; he just packs his shirt and goes visit some buddies at another base camp. Operations have become incredibly rag-tag; vehicles don't work for lack of maintenance; helicopters are just falling to the ground; airfields are falling apart. . . .
>
> It used to be they could get a couple of months of work out of new people but that is no longer the case. When new guys come into our company we rap how we've taken over and turn them on. . . ."

Subsequently, evidence has become available that indicates that this is by no means an isolated instance.[11] Such behavior reveals a

[11] See Col. Robert D. Heinl, Jr., "The Collapse of the Armed Forces," *Armed Forces Journal*, Vol. 108, No. 21 (June 7, 1971), 30–38.

collapse of discipline which could paralyze the armed forces if it spread widely.

Among the police in America itself, on the other hand, there has been so far no sign of this form of behavior. If anything, the opposite seems to be the case. Many newspaper accounts have reported the special delight rank-and-file police have taken in attacking groups and individuals whom they define—correctly in some cases, incorrectly in others—as revolutionaries. In several such cases the police have gone on a rampage. The police rampage, on the other hand, constitutes another form of the collapse of discipline. In the not so long run it could be dangerous for the forces of law and order themselves, because it alienates a very influential segment of respectable upper middle-class opinion, especially so when children from this sector are its victims. A police force that lacks the backing of influential opinion in the community is liable to become helplessly isolated. It might still be able to count on strong support from segments of the lower middle class, from "hard-hats" and the like. But if support were to come solely from that quarter, American society would indeed be well on the road to the war of all against all. And that does not mean revolution.

The processes just described are by no means irreversible. Armies have been restored to fighting trim many times by a combination of strategic retreat, a few well placed rewards, and a touch of disciplinary terror. Roughly the same is true of police forces. Furthermore it is clear by now that those in authority are aware of the revolutionary tactic of provoking repressive action, and are less likely to jump for the bait. The collapse of the instruments of violence remains a very long way off. And without control or neutralization of these instruments revolutionary movements do not have a shimmer of a ghost of a chance. If the revolutionaries persist in the tactics of desperation that became prominent by 1970, the bombing of buildings and the breaking of windows, in general an expression of diffuse rage against peripheral targets—they are liable to provide the forces of order with exactly the widespread public support they need. The nineteenth-century anarchist whom the desperate young imitate was actually the policeman's best friend. The anarchist managed to do just enough to frighten respectability without being able to cripple any vital social institution. To paraphrase Talleyrand, that is worse than criminal; it is mistaken.

Looking now at the lower classes we find in general more variety in the patterns that experience so far has revealed. Here it is important to distinguish between revolutions whose main base has been in the cities from those in the countryside.

An urban revolutionary mass provided the main destructive impetus in the French Revolution; the continental revolutions of 1848, particularly in the most important upheavals in Paris; the Paris Commune of 1871; the revolutions of 1905 and 1917 (both February and October) in Russia; the abortive revolution of 1918 in Germany. One process is common to these events: the transformation of a more or less atomized and diffuse urban plebs or of a proletariat into a politically active revolutionary mass.[12] These were all revolts of desperation, certainly not of rising expectations as some liberal theorists of revolution might lead one to anticipate.[13] Contrary to what one might expect on the basis of Leninist theory too, there is almost no evidence that prior organizational work and propaganda played a significant role and a good deal of evidence to the contrary. (Bolshevik organization did play a part in the October revolution of 1917 in Russia, but not in the more important February revolution that overthrew the Tsar and inaugurated a period of disorder upon which the Bolsheviks were able to capitalize.) Though the influence of prior forms of social organization, pre-existing habits and general outlook, is a topic that requires

[12] The term plebs is convenient for the *sans-culottes* and similar movements made up mainly of small shopkeepers, artisans, journeymen; proletariat for factory workers. There has yet to be a successful revolution (in the sense of seizing and holding power) in a country where the proletariat constituted a large segment of the lower classes.

[13] There is, on the other hand, an element of hope produced by some break in the ranks of the dominant classes, some sign, such as the Supreme Court's decision on educational desegregation in 1954, that changes are possible after all. In situations of utter hopelessness the response is more likely to be apathetic acceptance of "fate"; in extreme cases, found for example in concentration camps, people may give up and die in response to the general situation, not as a result of any single act of cruelty.

further investigation, I have come to suspect that it too plays a much less important role than immediate circumstances in creating a revolutionary mass. However, organization does play a part in sustaining revolutionary *élan* and making the mass politically effective, a state that apparently can be sustained for no more than a few years at most.

The main factors that create a revolutionary mass are a sudden increase in hardship coming on top of quite serious deprivations, together with the breakdown of the routines of daily life—getting food, going to work, etc.—that tie people to the prevailing order. The grievances of man as a consumer appear to be more important than those of man as a producer in providing fuel for such explosions. However, their proximate cause is the general breakdown of the flow of supplies into the city. If there are no goods upon which to work, artisans cannot go to their workshops, factory workers to their factories. (Or if they do, as in Petrograd in 1917, it may be mainly to stir each other up.) The final spark that sets off the conflagration among floating groups of desperate men (and sometimes even more desperate women who face even more directly the problem of getting food and keeping the household going) is likely to be some punitive act or threat by those in authority. If the authorities are already quarreling severely among themselves, the result may be a revolutionary upheaval, especially if the police and the army have ceased to be dependable. Otherwise there may be no more than a brief period of bloody disorder.

Hence in an urban lower-class population the creation of revolutionary solidarity resembles what happens when a bolt of lightning fuses some chunks of metal that happen to be close to each other into a single mass. Dramatic threat overcomes the atomization that the proliferation of different occupations creates in the city. This type of rapidly created solidarity breaks up again rather easily as individual interests reassert themselves. This breakup is not a matter of individual versus collective interests, at least not in any metaphysical sense. When a person joins a revolutionary crowd or even goes to a dramatic political demonstration, as an individual this person gains certain psychological satisfactions by seeing that other people have similar passions and by merging his own with those of the crowd. Under such circumstances there is a release of inhibitions, an opportunity to vent feelings of moral outrage, sentiments of moral superiority vis-à-vis those in authority to whom respect is ordinarily due, in other words a whole set of pleasures whose indulgence is ordinarily unsafe and imprudent. But the revolutionary crowd does not and cannot provide an adequate social mechanism for meeting the individual's other needs for food and shelter on a regular and recurring basis. Therefore the solidarity of the urban mass sustains itself only so long as it promises results. When all the food stores have been pillaged,[14] to speak metaphorically, the revolutionary crowd may turn on its own leaders or desert them. That is a theoretical maximum point, rarely approximated in real life, where revolutionary solidarity dissolves of its own accord. More often solidarity dissolves as more and more people return to the search for a private and more familiar everyday solution to their problems. There is a drift back to work. In the meantime a new authority armed with revolutionary legality may speed up the process with a judicious application of terror, accusing the leaders of the revolutionary crowd of anarchist and counter-revolutionary tendencies. Or, as happened in 1848, the forces of the old order may retain control of the army and be able to defeat the revolutionary crowd in bloody pitched battles at the barricades. In either case, whether revolutionary solidarity evaporates of its own accord or suffers violent suppression—or some combination of the two—once destroyed it is impossible to recreate it for a long time.[15]

So far then, urban revolutionary movements have been very short-lived, even if very important, agents of social change. There has never been any such thing as a long-term revolutionary mass

[14] Or all the land distributed, as W. Hinton points out for the area he observed in China. There are *some* similarities between urban and rural revolutionary movements.

[15] Twelve years of discouragement elapsed between the Russian revolutions of 1905 and 1917, the shortest interval between urban revolutionary outbreaks that I can recollect.

movement in an urban environment. That is, there has not been a movement with a mass basis that has sustained a revolutionary impetus for more than a generation. *A fortiori* there has never been a long-term urban revolutionary movement that has succeeded. Sooner or later, urban movements that start off with the aim of revolutionary change either turn into reformist movements or succumb in competition with reformism and pure trade unionism. That is what has happened in England, France, Germany, the United States, even to a great extent in Tsarist Russia. Among the many reasons for the failure of revolutionary movements to take deep root in an urban setting, the following seem to be the most important: 1) the very great division of labor and consequent atomization that work produces in the urban setting; 2) at least in industrial societies, a rising productivity that makes possible the granting of substantial benefits to the working classes, easing their social, legal, and cultural incorporation into the larger society; 3) the overwhelming political and economic power of the dominant group that closes off the prospect of revolutionary changes as long as this group remains reasonably united. All these factors drive urban revolutionary movements in a reformist direction.

The situation is, or rather can be, different in a rural setting, especially the kind conducive to successful peasant revolution. Though our concern here is with America, it is worth pointing out where the differences lie because an important current in American radicalism tries to apply, in an urban setting, strategy and tactics taken from rural movements.

The essential feature in peasant revolutions is the establishment of what are often called liberated areas. The Chinese Communist movement is the only one that has so far used this strategy successfully. It is actually a modernized version of one that has deep roots in specifically Chinese history and institutions.[16] The Chinese

---

[16] Unlike previous rebels Mao used peasant hostilities to create an entirely new social system based on new economic relationships. Another major innovation in the Chinese revolution is the effort to create artificially a revolutionary mass of the type described above *after* the seizure of power and use it to prevent the ossification of the regime. That has been one of the purposes of the Great Cultural Revolution. The Chinese are trying to

Communists were able to make a liberated area into what some American radicals might call a genuine counter-community. It was a place that provided real protection and security for its members. Here the peasants were free from the demands of the more rapacious tax collectors and landlords. In this fashion the liberated area provided the same kind of protection that a trade union does in a capitalist society. But, unlike the capitalist trade union, a liberated area undermines the prevailing "legal" order instead of supporting it. The liberated area can do this because it is self-sufficient, territorially independent of the legal central government, and more attractive to the mass of the population. As a matter of daily routine its members do not depend on anything except each other for food and for work. They are not tied to the existing order by depending upon it for jobs and through jobs for practically everything else.

Because of their stake in better conditions within the liberated area, peasants are likely to be more willing to furnish recruits to revolutionary armies than to government forces. Chinese experience demonstrates once again the independently crucial importance of revolutionary control over military force. Liberated areas, especially in the early stages, are not strong enough to defend themselves on their own. Both William Hinton's and Jan Myrdal's accounts give vivid evidence about the peasants' fear and hesitation to commit themselves to the Communist cause because they were afraid Chiang's troops might return, and the temporary demoralization that occurred when government troops did return. Without their isolation (the result of the Long March) and the fact that the Communists were able to detach a part of Chiang's army at the very beginning, it is highly unlikely that the Communist liberated areas could have survived at all.

It is easy enough to see that the essential conditions of a successful peasant revolution are almost impossible to reproduce in an

---

use Trotsky's permanent revolution as a mechanism for social adaptation and rejuvenation comparable to the way the democratic process is supposed to work in the West. It is unlikely that permanent revolution will do the job any better.

urban setting. The long period of prior disruption upon which the Chinese Communists built is something no industrial society would be likely to tolerate. The creation of a liberated area that is really independent culturally, economically, and politically would be extraordinarily difficult if not impossible. To sustain itself any oppositional political movement needs to be able to obtain for its members day-to-day benefits and protect them against reprisals. In modern industrial societies this necessity has so far always led to compromise with the existing order, to working within it to achieve piecemeal benefits. That is very clear in the history of trade unions. The same process has eroded the militancy of communist parties in Western countries, turning them into what amounts to social democratic parties. But let us examine the American situation more closely.

It is precisely this need for protection and continuing benefits that the many varieties of New Left revolutionaries and near-revolutionaries face enormous difficulties in meeting. As already pointed out, individual acts of terror turn most of the general population against the terrorists. Canadian experience with kidnaping and murder by the FLQ in the fall of 1970 also indicates that such acts make the general population and political leaders very willing to abandon civil liberties and accept a situation of martial law. Nor do campus uprisings and the momentary "liberation" of a university through a student riot, forms of revolt that have now subsided anyway though perhaps only temporarily, constitute steps towards setting up a real working community, a base from which influences can be expected to spread outwards and transform the existing social order.

To be sure, through the repressive response that this strategy (often quite deliberately) generates, it may help to increase the "surplus" population of utterly irreconcilable persons, contemptuous of any act or gesture that has about it the faintest odor of liberal democracy, and more or less immune to the blandishments of the affluent society. Though it is impossible to measure the size of this group, still almost entirely confined to young people, there are signs that this segment has been growing beyond its original base of college students. The question remains whether it can be organized in any way that is politically effective. It is even more doubtful that it can serve as some form of revolutionary base.

By now there has come into existence a scattering of communes and "kids' ghettos" that with considerable stretching of terminology could be called liberated areas. They are efforts to set up communities with considerable autonomy and more attractions than either the black ghetto or the rat race of so-called normal white society. This particular movement towards a distinct form of revolutionary community seems likely in practice to become and remain distinct from the larger society in no more than trivial ways, such as dress, eating habits, tastes in art and music and sexual practices, where deviance now scarcely threatens the existing order. The end result may be to leave this new form of social life as a tourist attraction that doesn't change anything. The surrounding society can proceed serenely in its normal path of growing investment in destruction. That is not to assert that it *will* proceed so serenely. The mass of the underlying population in an industrial society has enough fear of the prospects of liberation (and suppressed desires for it) to make excellent recruits for "spontaneous" violence and pogroms which would make the massacre of Saint Bartholomew's Day looks like a church picnic. Even if that does not happen, and the prevailing mixture of harassment and toleration continues, this form of counter-community is liable to remain parasitic upon the larger society. Though it may grow at the expense of its host, it is unlikely to be able to strike at the instruments of domination or to undermine them in the ways that liberated areas succeed in doing in a peasant revolution.

Communes, whether explicitly revolutionary or escapist or an uneasy mixture of the two, and adolescent ghettoes are, however, only one part of the current ferment. They may turn out to be the least important because they have to recruit a specific type of person—primarily though not exclusively youthful drop-outs—that the larger society remains unlikely to generate in sufficient numbers or at sufficiently crucial points in the social structure to provide the basis for qualitative change.

There are also numerous movements and attempts to achieve some version of what is loosely called community control. In urban areas this is a set of heterogeneous movements composed of two major elements. One element derives from a variety of efforts undertaken by black citizens 1) to protect themselves from the oppressive aspects of white control; 2) to extract as much as they can in the form of material benefits from the enveloping white society and 3) to establish autonomous local institutions. There are also some similar movements within predominantly white poor communities. These defensive searches for community do reach out beyond the world of adolescence and cover a very wide range of activities and undertakings. They include various efforts of black militants that are explicitly revolutionary, at least in their rhetoric. They also include attempts to gain control of the local school system, to establish local economic enterprises run by "the people," to widen employment opportunities in white enterprises that dominate the local area, and of course to extract from the welfare system those benefits to which they believe they are legally entitled. Thus their conception of revolution is much less immediate than that of white ex-student extremists.

The other component comes from white radicals, by no means all revolutionaries, in search of a wider constituency and greater political leverage. Their contribution appears to have been mainly in the realm of ideas along with some leaven of organizational skills. The ideas are primarily neo-anarchist ones to the effect that size and bureaucracy are the enemies of both human spontaneity and the possibility of making what one wants out of one's own life, or in just slightly more concrete terms, participating in those social decisions that determine the shape of the individual's life. At the same time there are contradictory echoes from the traditions of centralized socialism, such as an explicit awareness of the necessity for some degree of central economic planning.

Though it is impossible to predict what will happen to this curious amalgam, it is possible to point out certain problems that the movement for community control will have to solve if it is to have major political impact. Perhaps the most obvious one is its own political identity: does the movement really want to be revolutionary, and can it afford to be? This is the familiar issue of short-run benefits that hold the movement together versus long-run goals, in only a slightly different form. The contradiction appears vividly in two statements from the same short speech by the president of FIGHT, a community-based organization in Rochester, which he describes as "essentially a federation of black groups . . . that range from Black Panthers to black fraternities . . . essentially Uncle Tom in philosophy." At one point in his speech he asserted:

. . . "We are basically talking about redistribution of power. We're talking about changing the status quo, about disorganizing an organized structure. When talking about that, you're talking about acrimony, about confrontation, about setting up brand new guide lines.

"Therefore, it is incredible that anyone, today, would suggest to a group such as ours that we approach the white man on the grounds that we're going to be just like them and make their world more perfect by fitting into their mold. If that's all it's about, then forget it. . . ."

Only one paragraph further on the speech continued with the following remarks.

. . . "In Rochester, we had to explain to both the black and white community what FIGHT meant by 'profit.' Our definition is at variance with the traditional definition. For instance, if we take 10 welfare mothers off the welfare rolls . . . and these mothers work for us for a year, we state very emphatically in our profit and loss statement, under 'special category' that we saved the Monroe County Department of Social Services $50,000 because we took 10 people off welfare onto our payrolls. We have about 18 brothers working with us who were excons. If you go by the statistics, you'll find that about 75 per cent of the brothers who leave the slam get remanded in less than nine months. We found out that nobody with us went back to the slam; those who left us went on to better jobs. . . ."

. . . "We have these people off welfare and out of the slams getting training with us at Fight-On [a subsidiary of FIGHT which makes transformers, power supplies, and metal stampings] and then going on to Kodak and Xerox training programs. So we go back to Kodak and Xerox and say, 'Dig it man. Here we

are subsidizing *you* because we're training these people and send-
ing them on to you, pushing them into the mainstream, and not
getting any payback. So when we want to bind on some Kodak
machinery at less than cost we trade off.' Kodak sells us equipment at much less money. . . ."[17]

The type of gains that FIGHT made in this example, chosen for
its illustrative value, may be very well worth having in their own
right. It is also possible that in these general circumstances no
other strategy could accomplish anything at all, that the only alternative may be sterile revolutionary rhetoric. Yet it is about as plain
as can be that such a strategy is unlikely to lead towards any revolutionary transformation of American society.

Can *any* strategy along the lines of seeking community control
and community autonomy lead to revolutionary results? In his
thought-provoking *Stratégie ouvrière*, André Gorz, a close as-
sociate of J. P. Sartre, tried to resolve the general dilemma between
absorption into the prevailing order and rhetorical *attentisme* for a
mass uprising. His solution has considerable appeal not only because it purports to get around the difficulty that the "classical"
form of revolution may no longer be possible in advanced industrial societies, but also because it purports to avoid the consequence
of a repressive revolutionary dictatorship in the manner of a Stalin.
Essentially the strategy amounts to fighting (and winning) a series
of political and economic contests in which the workers step by
step gain increasing control over those decisions that determine
their own lives: more specifically the type, timing, and location of
industrial investment, a set of decisions now made in accord with
anticipations of profit. By winning these contests the workers
would step by step take control of the command posts in a modern
industrial society. Simultaneously they would deprive the capitalist
corporate elite of the possibility of operating the society to their
advantage and of putting up an effective resistance.

It is easy to see why this strategy, originally developed in the
context of the more militant labor movements of France and Italy,

[17] Cambridge Institute, Occasional Bulletin No. 2, June, 1970, *A Confer-
ence on Community Based Economic Development* (Cambridge, Mass.,
1970), 3, 9–10.

might seem to provide a workable formula for those American radicals seeking to become effective in alliance with movements towards community control. In the American context industrial workers do not seem promising because so many of them want bread-and-butter benefits within the capitalist framework. On the other hand, the movement towards community control explicitly seeks to change the distribution of power and the way human beings live their lives. Thus it appears to the proponents of this general line of thinking that in the movement for community control American society provides a ready-made audience and potentially growing base for action. Nevertheless, there are, I think, powerful reasons for rejecting this variant of revolutionary optimism as well.

Quite aside from the consideration that the corporate elites can hardly be expected to be so stupid as to fail to notice what is taking place at quite an early stage, there are reasons to doubt that the strategy is inherently transferable from workers to what is loosely called "the community." In the first place, "the community" is a rhetorical term for congeries of individuals with very different outlooks and interests. By itself that is not wholly decisive: the articulate and energetic individuals who can swallow scruples about genuine participation for the sake of larger ideals could conceivably come to dominate "the community" and act as its politically effective spokesmen. In the process, however, much of what is morally attractive about these movements would inevitably vanish, as usually happens in the course of achieving political success and responsibility. Much more important is the consideration that in order for some such strategy to work, "the community" has to be able to threaten to withhold something that the corporate elites want, or to produce situations that the corporate elites do not want. Here unionized industrial workers have an enormous advantage in that they can withhold their labor power by a strike. As far as I can perceive, "the community" has nothing comparable that it can withhold. Perhaps it might have this power if there were enough community operated factories. But then the communities would be woven into the larger social fabric through all sorts of ties that create a reluctance to use this weapon. Nor is it easy to see what they can produce that the corporate elites do not want except a certain amount of riots and disorder. These are not something that can be turned on and off at will in accord with strategic and tactical requirements; they happen for other reasons. Furthermore, as long as the elites remain reasonably united and in control of the main means of violence, popular disorders on an intermittent and local scale remain quite easy to control and contain.

There are other and actually more fundamental criticisms to be made of the strategy of revolutionary change through community control. These have to do with inherent weaknesses in the anarchist tradition. As pointed out in an earlier chapter, the mere existence of a set of autonomous human communities living in the same social space is enough to set in motion potentially destructive rivalries in the form of coalitions and counter-coalitions as the separate units seek a margin of security against the behavior of a potential opponent. I have also tried to show why abundance or the solution of the problem of scarcity, even if that were possible under a new cultural definition of abundance, would not prevent these rivalries from coming into existence. There are also strong reasons for doubting whether the solution of the problem of scarcity is at all possible on a world-wide scale. No amount of cultural redefinition can make real hunger pangs disappear. That leaves humanity with the problem of rich and poor autonomous communities with all the explosive potentialities such a situation contains. There is no reason to linger on these points now. They are issues that would arise only after the revolution anyway. Fortunately some of the most intelligent and thoughtful radicals are well aware of them. Conceivably they might hit upon solutions. Even if they do not, as seems to me likely, the effect of the movement towards community control may be to alter the field of contending forces within which major economic and political decisions now have to be made, and in a way that would reduce very considerably the causes of human suffering and indignity. In other words, the movement may act as the radical fire under liberal reforms—a bitter disappointment to many of its proponents, but of considerable benefit to humanity.

So far we have been discussing revolutionary and near-revolutionary forms of change in American society based on the creation

of mass support for these changes prior to some kind of violent outbreak and the collapse of the existing order. We have seen that it is
vastly more difficult to build this support within the framework of
a modern industrial society than it is in at least some varieties of a
peasant society, that the embryo of a new social order cannot easily form within the womb of the old one under modern conditions.
We have also noticed the crucial part that the military forces and the
police can play, that no violent transformation can possibly take
place unless the insurgent elements can neutralize or gain control
of the instruments of violence.

There remains at least one other possible contingency: a major
breakdown or collapse of the political apparatus *without* prior mass
support for serious social changes. Such a collapse might provide
the opening for a revolutionary takeover by some tiny but resolute
minority in quasi-Leninist fashion. Though by no means an immediate prospect, such an eventuality does seem to me a distinct
possibility. In the light of obstacles to other forms of change,
including those within the democratic framework, there is even
some reason for suspecting that collapse without prior mass support could be the most likely possibility. It is also one that a segment of young American radicals evidently seeks. In any case this
kind of collapse constitutes the maximum goal of the tactic of
radicalization through disruption.

There are some good historical and sociological reasons too for
holding that such a collapse might both occur and permit a revolutionary takeover. As pointed out above, in an urban setting the
creation of a revolutionary mass is a quite rapid transformation.
Fundamentally it comes about through the breakdown of the supply of goods and services upon which a city is dependent. In recent
years there have been numerous partial breakdowns from a variety
of causes that have nothing to do with revolution as ordinarily conceived, such as strikes or near-strikes by key employees: police,
fire, sanitation workers, teachers, and postal workers. They have
exposed the vulnerability of the city to disruption.[18] One of the

---

[18] In this connection there arises the interesting question whether a modern industrial society is more vulnerable to disruption than pre-industrial

most threatening and sociologically interesting possibilities is a repetition of the electrical power failure that affected much of the Northeast not so long ago. Beneath the good humor of the last blackout there was an undertone of anxiety, not necessarily eased by frequent broadcasts to assure the population that the Pentagon was functioning normally and felt sure there was no emergency. Electricity means even more to a modern city than the supply of wheat to eighteenth-century Paris. France in May, 1968 demonstrated the vulnerability of a whole modern industrial state to spontaneous and yet concerted disruption, as well as some of the obstacles in the way of carrying it through to a revolutionary conclusion. Though a revolutionary mass can form in a modern industrial society and can paralyze the society briefly, it cannot take power on its own. For a revolution to take place there must also exist some group, such as the Russian Bolsheviks in 1917, that knows what it wants to accomplish and that is willing to seize power in the midst of chaos and exercise it ruthlessly to restore order.

It would be a curious historical irony if the anarcho-syndicalist dream of the general strike and revolution somehow came true, several generations after the theory behind it had passed into the museum of social history and in a country such as the United States where it has flourished only very briefly. It is not out of the question that further attempts along these lines may be made and even that one on a big scale might induce some form of temporary collapse. But it seems to me highly unlikely that the attempt could

---

ones. Since there is a much greater interdependence among the parts of an industrial society, it is easy to conclude that it is much more vulnerable. However, the experience of Germany and Japan under allied bombing in the Second World War points toward an opposite conclusion. Large cities can be virtually destroyed without bringing about a general collapse of the social order. Leningrad too continued to function as a city when almost totally cut off from the rest of the Soviet Union by the German armies. Those who are doing the disrupting, either foreign enemies or revolutionaries, evidently cannot succeed unless they can destroy or capture the key centers of the government, a point Blanqui recognized more than a century ago.

turn out the way its proponents wish. It is almost certain to have quite the opposite result.

In the first place, even if black and white radicals could work together long enough to get the process started off, in the American context it seems highly unlikely that they could persuade workers in essential services to join them for quite some time to come. There is little likelihood that they could neutralize both the police and the army. There is a less obvious and perhaps even more important consideration. Should disorder somehow proceed far enough to create a revolutionary mass, would its temper and objectives be at all similar to that of the *sans-culottes* in eighteenth-century Paris, or Russian workers, and—for a brief moment—central European workers, at the end of World War I? The urban masses in these situations had undergone considerable hardships for some time. When the bonds of the status quo snapped under sudden additional strains, there were many in the mass who were already angry at what was clearly to them an oppressive social order. They were emotionally ready to try something new, to support leaders who promised something new, though what evidence we have indicates fairly clearly that the masses had no more than very vague notions about what the new society should be. It is conceivable that the black population, the real mass in many major American cities, might display a similar temper in the course of a general collapse. The white population, on the other hand, while it might get very angry, would be rather more likely to be angry at disorder and chaos, to throw its support to whatever person or group promised to get the electricity turned on, the gas pumps and television sets working, the stores open. By and large it seems safe to predict that the groups angry enough to produce disruption would be on opposite sides of the barricades: police and other city employees on the one side, blacks, student radicals, a few intellectuals on the other.

Hence any such major disruption would very likely result in martial law or worse. Unless events and trends that no one can now foresee intervene to generate both widespread support for a revolutionary break and a more passive willingness to go along with it, any temporary collapse within the next twenty or thirty years would probably have utterly tragic consequences. Even if it succeeds in taking power, a revolution that tries to remold society against the mores and folkways of the mass of the population must turn to terror and propaganda on a gigantic scale in order to stay in control. In America a black dictatorship of the proletariat or even a black and white version—something as far as I am aware no one takes very seriously—might have poetic justice on its side, but practically nothing else. It would almost certainly be a failure.

What is it that we mean by the success or failure of a revolutionary movement? I have deliberately saved this question for the end. Actually there is no such thing as complete success or complete failure, only differences of degree. Yet these differences of degree have decisive importance. A revolution that is crushed by its enemies we can call a failure even if its legend survives as an inspiration (perhaps a thoroughly misleading one) for later generations. On the other hand, taking power and even staying in power for a couple of generations are not by themselves sufficient grounds for us to call a revolution successful. From a longer-run standpoint it is necessary to define success as making some lasting contribution to human freedom.

So far, I think it is fair to assert that no radical revolutionary movements have made such contributions on their own, at least not yet. They have made them only as part of the "bourgeois" or "liberal" revolutionary movements—the great surges of the Puritan and French revolutions and our own Civil War, which belong to an historical epoch that is now drawing to a close. The first revolution that took power mainly as the result of a radical thrust, the Bolshevik Revolution, turned into a vicious form of oppression that has yet to be shaken off. In China the issue is still doubtful. I believe very firmly that unless future radical movements can somehow synthesize the achievements of liberalism with those of revolutionary radicalism, the results for humanity will be tragic.

Given a commitment to minimizing the social causes of human misery and allowing human beings to obtain happiness in a variety of ways, some form of democratic and humane socialism may well be the most desirable set of social arrangements. But the obstacles are staggering. Where socialism has come to power by revolutionary means it has done so in backward countries and under conditions that have largely destroyed what humane aspects there were in the original tradition. In its effort to achieve power by peaceful and legal means in advanced industrial countries, socialism has had to compromise so deeply with the crimes of law and order that it has lost its capacity for bringing about fundamental change. The collaboration between the German socialists and the General Staff during the First World War was only one of the more dramatic instances of this general trend. Communists too have become parties of law and order, most notably in France. In American society the prospects for any synthesis between the liberal and radical traditions are dim, the prospects for any transformation of American society by purely peaceful and democratic means dimmer still.

These are the reasons behind a very somber sense of the world to come. A somber view is not, on the other hand, a passive and fatalist one. One task of human thought is to try to perceive what the range of possibilities may be in a future that always carries on its back the burden of the present and the past. Though that is not the only task of the intellectual, it is a very important and very difficult one. No one can do it with complete success. Only those with a religious conviction of the infallibility of their own beliefs can take seriously the notions of inevitable catastrophe and inevitable utopia. To give up such consolations is to become really serious about a very deadly and very serious world.

Index

Classes, dominant (*Cont.*)
power, 14–15, 175; and liberalism, 88–89; splits in, 174–175. *See also* Elites
Clifford, Clark: 148 (note 52)
Cognitive dissonance: 153 (note 2)
Cold war: 137, 139
Collins Radio: 141 (note 46)
Communes: 20, 73–76, 183
Communists: Chinese, 65, 180–182; French, 193. *See also* Bolsheviks
Community control: 183–186
Conservatism: 152–154
Corporations: international, 123 (note 21), 129 (note 30); and military expenditures, 139–144; and social responsibility, 162; and unmanageable surplus, 126–130
Costs: nature of concept, 10–13
Cruelty, social role: 24–26, 27–28, 38–39, 82
Cuba: 146
Cultural relativism and neutrality: 11, 51–52, 137

Davie, M. R.: 19 (note 6)
DeGaulle, Charles: 21 (note 7)
De-industrialization: 75, 123, 133, 173
Depression of 1929: 106, 129, 138
Determinism, avoiding: 10
Dominican Republic: 146
Douglas, Mary: 24 (note 11)
Doyle, Michael: 122 (note 20)
Dubos, René: 41 (note 1), 43 (note 2)
Durkheim, Émile: 58, 171 (note 10)

Ehrlich, Anne H.: 107 (note 4)
Ehrlich, Paul R.: 107 (note 4)
Einstein, Albert: xiv (note)
Elites and elitism: 63–66, 91, 92, 108, 155, 160; in American society, 108, 131, 160–162, 163, 174–175, 187–188. *See also* Classes
Engels, Friedrich: 49
England: 124, 155–156, 160, 161, 165, 180
Expenditures, government: educational, 109; military, 106, 108–109, 119, 128 (note 28), 129, 140, 156; social insurance, 109; veterans, 109
Exploitation: 53–54; and imperialism, 116, 124; and liberalism, 165
Exports, U.S.: 119. *See also* Trade

Fascism: 138, 152. *See also* Nazis
Festinger, Leon: 153 (note 2)
FIGHT: 185–186
Foreign investment, U.S.: 123 (note 21), 124, 125 (note 23), 128 (note 28), 129 (note 30)
Foreign policy, United States: China, 114–115; counterrevolutionary nature, 106–107, 117, 174; and domestic reform, 166–167; economic aspects, 116, 118–125, 138; India, 114; Latin America, 116; Middle East, 116
Forrestal, James: 138
France, Anatole: 62
France: 124, 186–187, 190, 193
Frazer, J. G.: 55
French Revolution: 23, 24, 28, 29, 155, 170, 177, 180, 192
Freud: 1, 23, 58
Frustration: 152–153

General Dynamics Corporation: 141 (note 46)
General Motors: 140, 142 (note 48)
Germany: 124, 193; failure of revolution in, 30, 177, 180
Goldman, Marshall I.: 44 (note 3)
Gombrich, E. H.: 6 (note 4)
Gordon, Robert J.: 128 (note 28)

198

Latin America: 116
League of Nations: 34
Legitimacy: and authority, 23, 53–55, 56–57; decay of, 171–174; of opposition, 28, 88–91; revolutionary succession, 70
Lenin: 25, 39, 70, 168
Leningrad: 189 (note 18)
Leontief, Wassily: 122 (note 20), 143
Liberalism: 19, 88–91; in capitalist democracy, 111–112, 182; hypocrisy, 98; -with-a-difference, 156, 159, 164–167
Liberated areas: 180–182, 183
Lieberson, Stanley: 139, 140, 141 (note 47), 142 (note 48), 143, 144 (note 50)
Lockheed Corporation: 141 (note 46)
LTV, Inc.: 141 (note 46)

McDonnell Corporation: 141 (note 46)
Machiavelli, Niccolò: 84
Magdoff, Harry: 107 (note 4), 118, 119, 122, 124, 129 (note 30)
Maier, Charles S.: 135 (note 36), 139 (note 41)
Malinowski, Bronislaw: 56
Manganese: 120
Mao Tse-tung: 180 (note 16)
Marcuse, Herbert: xii, 64 (note 10), 81–82, 118, 133
Martin, John: 14 (note 1)
Martin-Marietta Corporation: 141 (note 46)
Marx, Karl: 29, 51, 58, 71 (note 16), 168, 169
Mbuti: 16–19
Merleau-Ponty, M.: 39 (note 18)
Middle East: 116
Military: and business, 137–141; control over, 14–15, 175–176, 189;

expenditures: 106, 108–109, 119, 127, 128 (note 28), 129, 140, 156; expenditures and corporate income, 139, 141 (note 48)
Millis, Walter: 138
Mills, C. Wright: 131
Misery: changes in perception of, 12–13; and genius, xv; and intellectual freedom, 79–81; social roles, 23, 24–29, 39; unitary nature, 1–2, 5, 11, 24. See also Cruelty
Modernization: 42. See also Industrialization
Moore, Barrington, Jr.: 64 (note 10), 82 (note 3)
Moral issues and politics: 3–5, 7, 10, 22–23, 38, 57
Morgenstern, Oskar: 142 (note 48)
Mosca, Gaetano: 65
Myrdal, Jan: 181
Myths, political: 105–106, 171

Napoleonic Wars: 155
Nazis: 24, 29, 30
Negroes in United States: 108, 110–111, 191; community control movement, 183–184
Netherlands, Revolt of the: 28, 170
New Deal: 106
New Left: 19, 182
Newport News Shipbuilding: 141 (note 46)
Non-literate societies: 14, 16–20; aggression in, 17–18; and sense of injustice, 56
Northrup Aviation: 141 (note 46)

O'Brien, Conor Cruise: 114
Order: post-revolutionary, 65–66, 193; need for, 20, 44–46, 62, 64, 73–76, 83, 84 (note 5)